Now It Is Time

NOW IT IS TIME

Lois Heathman Roberts

BROADMAN PRESS

Nashville, Tennessee

BV
3427
S65
R6
1983
c.3

© Copyright 1983 • Broadman Press
All rights reserved.
4272-28
ISBN: 0-8054-7228-2
Dewey Decimal Classification: 266.092
Subject Headings: SMITH, LUCY // MISSIONS—CHINA
Library of Congress Catalog Card Number: 82-71221
Printed in the United States of America

Unless otherwise stated, Scripture quotations are
from the King James Version of the Bible.

Scripture quotations marked (NASB) are from the
New American Standard Bible. Copyright © The Lockman Foundation,
1960, 1962, 1963, 1971, 1972, 1973, 1975.
Used by permission.

All letters or portions of letters quoted are from:
Missionary Correspondence of
Miss Lucy E. Smith
Foreign Mission Board
Richmond, Virginia

**To my nephew, Steve Calhoun
and other
young people
serving on the
foreign mission field**

Special thanks to:
Elizabeth G. Smith,
for her taping the information
from Miss Lucy,
and Effie Katherine Root,
Miss Lucy's sister

Kirke White,
Manager, Records, Repographics
and Mail Section,
Foreign Mission Board

Dr. George Hays,
Director for East Asia

Miss Catherine Walker
and Mrs. Johnni Johnson Scofield,
former missionaries to the Orient

Contents

1. Lucy Elizabeth　9
2. Waiting on the Lord　15
3. Across the Pacific　23
4. First Years in China　28
5. Interrupted by War　36
6. Communists in China　46
7. Decision to Go to Tokyo, 1951　55
8. Furlough Interrupted　66
9. Return to Tokyo, 1959　71
10. Hong Kong　79
11. Retirement　88
12. Going Home　93
    Epilogue　95

1
Lucy Elizabeth

The long summer had ended three days before. On September 24, 1898, the little log house near Charleston, Missouri, was filled with an aura of happiness and contentment. That morning, a little girl was born to Ida Stark and Edmund Kirby Smith.

Interested relatives were anxious to hear about the first grandchild in the family. An aunt asked, "What are we going to call her?"

"Lucy Elizabeth," her father answered proudly. He could not imagine that one day people in America and in the Orient would know and love Lucy Elizabeth Smith.

Mr. Smith farmed and planned for the new home he wanted to build for his family. Two years later, the new house by the highway was completed. It was located near the community school. The school's only teacher lived with the Smiths during the school term.

The family increased to include twins Harry and Herbert, Effie Katherine, and Carl. Herbert died in infancy.

Although Lucy was just two years older than the twins, she loved helping to take care of them. One summer morning, Mrs. Smith put the twins and Lucy on the front porch to play. The twins were beginning to crawl, so Mrs. Smith turned to Lucy and said, "Now watch them for me." A short time later, she heard all three children screaming. She made a mad dash to the door to see what dire tragedy had befallen them. At the door, she could see the problem. She had to stop and laugh. Each of the boys had started toward the edge of the porch in a different direction. Lucy, true to her trust, had grabbed the shirttail of each and was holding on for dear life, screaming for help.

The Smiths attended a church nearby. Services were on a part-time basis because several denominations used the building.

When Lucy was ten, the family moved to Edmond, Oklahoma. Their furniture and other household goods were shipped to their new home, and the family traveled by train. The children were excited about their new home and their first train ride. Mr. Smith felt the children would be better behaved and much happier if they had ample rest, so he made arrangements for them to have a compartment on the train. The next morning a passenger in the diner remarked on how well behaved the children were. Mr. Smith thanked her as he smiled knowingly at his wife. He was gratified that he had done what he felt best for his family. Upon arrival in Edmond, Mr. and Mrs. Smith joined the First Baptist Church. For the first time Lucy and the other children were able to attend church regularly.

The next year, during a revival service, Lucy gave her heart to the Lord. Because she was eleven years old and had a limited religious background, Mr. and Mrs. Smith encouraged her to wait for baptism and church membership until they felt she realized the importance of her decision.

Two years later, Lucy again responded to the pastor's invitation. This time she joined the church and was baptized. She said, "After that, there was never any question about my conversion or experience with the Lord."

Lucy was fortunate to have a dedicated Sunday School teacher who helped her and encouraged her. While still a teenager, Lucy began working with the younger children at church.

After graduating from the eighth grade, Lucy attended Edmond Normal School (now Central State University). The family moved to Oklahoma City, and Lucy transferred to Central High School. Lucy and her parents also moved their church membership to Olivet Baptist Church. Olivet was to remain Lucy's home church.

Lucy had felt for some time that God had called her to be a missionary to China. Her pastor encouraged her in her decision to attend Oklahoma Baptist University in Shawnee, after graduation from high school in 1917.

With mixed emotions, Lucy packed her trunk for college. She looked forward to the exciting days ahead, but she had never been away from home for such a long period before. As friends came by, they would tease, "You will be so homesick; we'll see you soon."

Knowing she needed to train for the work she would do in China, she studied hard. There were no restrictions on the number of hours one carried, and Lucy took as many hours as she felt she could manage. But even with many hours given to study, Lucy found time for fun and friends. Some close friendships were formed in those days.

The girls at OBU wore uniforms, and the dormitory hours were strictly enforced. The dean of women expected the young women to be very ladylike, but she did want them to be able to express their spirit. She suggested, "When your team is playing, wave your handkerchiefs and call 'press them fiercely, Boys.'"

Lucy started college in September and stayed until

Thanksgiving break, since transportation was too expensive and inconvenient to go home on weekends. She could truthfully boast to all her friends at home, "I never did get homesick once."

After her trip home, Lucy went back to school to stay until Christmas. She admitted, "When I went back I nearly died, I got so homesick. I thought I couldn't stay." But she did. After Christmas, she went back to finish the second semester.

Because of her father's health, the family moved to Tahlequah, Oklahoma. Lucy moved with them and spent the summer there. In the fall, it seemed rather foolish to go back to OBU when there was a junior college in Tahlequah. Finances had to be considered, and living at home while going to school would certainly be cheaper. She enrolled in Northeast Normal and attended there a full year. She graduated in the spring of 1919.

During that school year, Lucy's family moved back to Oklahoma City. Her father's health precluded her going back to school, and she got a job teaching school in a consolidated district out from Mangum, Oklahoma.

Teaching school was far more than just teaching academics. Talents she had not expected to use were needed on several occasions. Besides her regular classes, she coached basketball and taught drama.

At one time during the winter, there was so much snow the buses couldn't run. Only the hardy souls who rode horseback ventured in. School was closed. The school play had been advertised to run the next week, so rehearsals were absolutely necessary. The cast came in on horseback, and rehearsals went on in true theatrical tradition.

One day after play practice, a cast member invited Miss

Lucy to go home with her. They all began to insist and said they could practice there. Miss Lucy consented before she realized her only transportation was a horse. One of the students gallantly offered to ride with another boy and let her have his horse. The evening was so successful that she gladly accepted an invitation to another student's home the next day.

The students brought a horse to Miss Lucy's house for her to ride. She finished her chores at home and started out to the student's home later in the afternoon. The horse was gentle, and she was thoroughly enjoying the ride. Miss Lucy had directions to the student's home: cross the railroad tracks, turn left, and go about a mile. When Miss Lucy came to the railroad crossing, suddenly the horse turned and raced down the tracks. With hair, arms, and feet standing out, Miss Lucy yelled at the horse and pulled on the reins, but to no avail. The horse took a sudden turn, went through a gate, and stopped in front of the house. She simply took a short cut. Rehearsals were limited to the school after that experience.

The Wednesday after school was out in the spring, Miss Lucy returned home. She was glad to see her family again. Her father said, "Lucy, I want you to go with me to my office tomorrow morning."

Early the next morning Lucy unpacked her things. Then she and her father went down to his office to talk.

He very calmly said, "Lucy, the doctor tells me I'm not going to live much longer. I can't work any more, but my boss has offered my job to you if you will take it."

Years later, Miss Lucy slowly related the sad details. "He gave me a check for all the money he had and told me about his business and how to take care of things. The next day he got worse. The doctor told me, 'He will either starve to death or strangle to death.' I prayed, 'Oh Lord, I don't know which would be worse . . . I can't stand either one . . . please, nothing like that.' He died the next night."

Mr. Smith's death in 1922 and assuming responsibility for the family seemed to be the end of Lucy's schooling and her plans to go to China.

Once when looking back on that event, Miss Lucy said, "His death seemed the end of the way for me as far as missions were concerned. But the Lord always has a plan, usually so much better than any we might have thought or dreamed about. I worked in the business world until the Lord said, 'Now, it is time for you to finish your education and preparation for what I have for you to do.'"

2
Waiting on the Lord

The next eight years were pleasant but certainly not what Lucy had planned for her life. Effie Katherine was about half finished with her nurse's training when their father died. Harry had been in the navy and was living in Oklahoma City. Carl was still in high school. Mrs. Smith was not well, so Lucy felt she had no other choice but to stay home and work.

John Huff was pastor at Olivet Baptist Church, and Lucy helped out at the church when she had time. Her office was downtown. She walked to and from work, without even thinking of owning a car. In those days she said, "No one ever thought about being afraid. I walked home from the office or the church at night without any thought of fear."

Early every morning Lucy had her devotional time in her office before starting the day's work. At the end of eight years, during her devotional time, the Lord spoke to Lucy. She said, "One morning the Lord said to me just as clearly as could be, 'Now, it is time for you to go back to school and prepare to do what I've asked you to do.'

"When the Lord called me at fifteen, I knew he was mistaken because I couldn't do anything. I didn't think then I would ever get to college. Now, I knew I had no choice." She wrote to the Foreign Mission Board to keep them informed of her plans.

Lucy began to investigate her college credits to see how

much school lay ahead. Fortunately, Effie Katherine had finished her nurse's training and had gone to work. This helped with the finances at home. Lucy wanted to go to Louisville for seminary training. Two years of seminary and two more years of college made appointment as a missionary sound far away. The years were going by, and her age was increasing along with them. She received approval to go to school in Louisville. There were no limits on the number of credits a student could take if her grades were all right. Lucy learned that with the two college credits she had earned in high school plus the extras she had taken in OBU and Tahlequah, she could finish college with one year and three summer's work.

Louisville had been her mother's home, and relatives still lived there. So Lucy moved her family to Louisville. Effie Katherine got a job in Speed, Indiana, which was just across the river from Louisville. The family was together on weekends, and it was a happy time for all of them.

After one year in Louisville, Lucy became quite ill. The doctor insisted a tonsillectomy was absolutely necessary. In spite of her insistence that she had never had a sore throat, the doctor proceeded with plans for the tonsillectomy.

The operation itself was rather uneventful, but that night Lucy started hemorrhaging. Recuperation took longer than she had expected, so she was not able to work during the summer as she had planned.

Lucy graduated from school in Louisville in May and went back to OBU to finish her college work. Effie Katherine took a position in Muncie, Indiana. Mrs. Smith and Carl moved back to Oklahoma City with Lucy. The family once more joined Olivet Baptist Church.

Lucy was to participate in the spring graduating exercises, even though she thought she would not finish until the end of the summer term. She was surprised but elated when the dean called her into his office and said, "Lucy, we have your transcript here. You don't have to go to school this summer. You already have enough hours to fill all the requirements for graduation."

After attending OBU during the summer of 1926 and 1927, and the Woman's Missionary Union Training School for Christian Workers during the school years 1926-27 and 1927-28, Lucy had completed her education and was at long last ready to go to China.

The Foreign Mission Board suffered during the economic depression of the late 1920's. There just was no money available to send more missionaries at that time. This delay was extremely disappointing. Surely the Lord would not have called her if he had not meant for her to go. Why had he allowed her to go through all those years of waiting and preparation for nothing? Knowing she was not to question the way God works, Lucy decided to get a job and wait on the Lord for whatever he wanted her to do.

Dr. Naney was pastor at Olivet now. He asked Lucy to work in the church office while his secretary was on a month's vacation. He added, "I have every reason to believe that she is planning to resign. Why don't you take her job?"

"No, thank you," Lucy answered quickly. "I will take the job temporarily, but only until the end of her vacation."

The music and education director, as well as the secretary, resigned within a few weeks. A week went by without any further discussion between Lucy and Dr. Naney about a permanent job. The next Monday night the deacons met. Dr. Naney walked into the office on Tuesday morning and said, "It's all yours. We voted to hire you."

"I told you in the beginning, I wasn't interested . . . I don't want to talk about it," Lucy stammered.

"Why? Do you not want to work with me?" Dr. Naney questioned.

"That isn't the problem. I've grown up in this church. I'm just *Lucy* to young and old. I wouldn't think about taking it."

"I know you can't handle the music, except to see that they have it, but you can do everything the educational director does," explained Dr. Naney. "You will pray about it, won't you?"

"No, I don't think I will."

As she recalled the story years later, Lucy chuckled and said, "Of course, if you're a Christian, you can't just throw it off. So, it took the Lord about three weeks to convince me he knew what he was doing.

"I had other job offers. When my class graduated, the Foreign Mission Board told us there would be other openings from time to time, and we could only hope it would not be long. Other jobs seemed to fade into insignificance as the summer went on. I finally said, 'Yes' to Dr. Naney and settled down to work."

The next eight years were very happy years. Obviously being "Just Lucy" was an asset. Not everything went exactly as she liked and there were problems to face, but the church work went well.

Speaking of that time Miss Lucy said, "We did many things during those years. The association had its first Vacation Bible School. We did it by the book, and boy, did we work."

The school started with a parade on Saturday and lasted four weeks. The volunteer workers had to do all of their own posters and all of the material from kindergarten through Intermediates (as they were called then). The superintendent of each department, with the help of the Intermediates, made

Waiting on the Lord 19

many beautiful things from whatever material they could find.

Several times during those years, Lucy received word from the Foreign Mission Board about an opening. After praying about it, it didn't seem the right thing for her to do. The years passed, and it seemed she would never go to the mission field.

One day while Lucy was still working at Olivet, Dr. Naney went to the parsonage next door to the church and asked Mrs. Naney, "I can't find Lucy. Do you know where she is?"

"Yes," answered Mrs. Naney. "She is in the back bedroom crying."

"Why?" asked Dr. Naney.

"Today is her birthday. She has reached the age beyond which the Board will not appoint anyone to the foreign mission field," said Mrs. Naney. Lucy thought her chance was gone forever, but God was still working on his plan for her.

In October, 1935, Lucy received a letter from the Foreign Mission Board saying that Dr. M. Theron Rankin wanted to meet her at the Oklahoma State Convention in November. In talking with Dr. Naney about it, she said, "I'm not sure I want to go. I've been disappointed so many times."

Dr. Naney said, "I'm going to write that Board and tell them to leave you alone. They just keep you disturbed about what to do."

"Now, don't do that. Let's just wait and see what the Lord works out for me to do," interjected Lucy.

In November, Lucy went to the convention in Enid. Juliet Mather, young people's director, for the Woman's Missionary Union and Berta K. Spooner, state WMU secretary, were there. They found Lucy and told her Theron Rankin had arrived. Lucy asked, "Who's he?"

"He is a missionary from China who has just been elected

to a new position. He is the secretary for the Orient. He needs an assistant, and your name has been suggested. Of course, I told them you could do it," answered Juliet Mather.

Dr. Rankin did meet Lucy before the service that night and made an appointment to meet her the next morning to discuss some plans.

They talked for two hours or more the next morning. He said, "I don't expect you to give me an answer right now. I realize this is new to you. It's new to me. This is a new position. Our mission work has just been divided into three fields: the Orient, Europe and the Middle East, Africa and South America."

Later, recalling the incident, Lucy said, "I sat through the whole convention, but I'm not sure how much of it I heard."

Miss Mather and Mrs. Spooner knew about the discussion and were on needles and pins for some information. Lucy had made no decision, so there was nothing to say. After the services that night Lucy and her three roommates went to their room. The other three went to sleep, but sleep evaded Lucy.

She talked it over with God. She prayed, "Now, Lord, I don't know anything about this man. I don't know anything about this job. I don't know what I'm supposed to do if I go, but I will try to find out something about him and see if I think I can work with him. I'll talk to other people and ask questions, and then we'll see."

The Lord answered her, "But I know him, and I know you." Then Lucy was able to go to sleep. No further question lingered in her mind. The matter was settled.

The next day she found Dr. Rankin and said, "Let's go somewhere and talk." She told him exactly what had transpired the night before and added, "I'm ready. I'll go with you."

He admitted, "Well, I'm surprised, but very pleased. Last

night you didn't seem sure at all. But after talking with you, I knew you were the one for the position."

Dr. Rankin was not going back to China until July, and Lucy would not be appointed until April, so they decided not to tell anyone for a while.

Around noon one of Oklahoma's sudden storms brought heavy winds and rain. It struck with such fury, convention leaders decided to close the meeting as soon as possible after lunch.

Right after lunch, Dr. Rankin approached Lucy and said, "I've changed my mind. I'm going to tell them you are going back with me."

"But you can't tell them," she said. "My pastor doesn't know anything about it; my family has heard nothing; my church doesn't know. You can't tell them."

He said, "That's why I want to tell it. It's stormy. People are worried. Some of them are leaving. We need something to close out the convention, and I think this is it." He explained, "All I will do is introduce you and tell them what our plans are."

Arguing at that point was obviously useless, so Lucy consented. They went into the auditorium together.

Dr. Rankin stood on the platform and told those gathered what had happened. Then, he introduced Lucy and added, "Now Miss Smith has something she would like to say."

When telling about this moment, Miss Lucy said, "I could have choked him. I hadn't even thought of such a thing. I said a few words, but I don't know what they were. As soon as we were finished, we headed for home.

"Of course, I told Mother as soon as I got home. She cried as if her whole world had changed, so I didn't sleep again that night.

"Saturday morning I went down to the church to talk with Dr. Naney. He was surprised, even though he knew Theron was talking to me about my going.

"When he made the announcement in church Sunday morning, you never saw such weeping and wailing. People were surprised. They asked what I would do about Mother.

"There were many decisions to make. God has never promised to make things easy for us, but he has promised to go with us all the way. With his help, we were able to make the necessary arrangements. Effie Katherine and her husband, Clifton Root, moved back to Oklahoma City to be near Mother.

"I found the Lord had a plan for me all the time, and now he was ready for me to go to the field where he had called. I was appointed to the Orient."

Lucy was appointed to be an associate to Dr. Rankin in the headquarters offices for the Orient, located in Shanghai.

3
Across the Pacific

Lucy had mixed emotions as she left home to sail to China on October 10, 1936.

"I was thrilled that I was getting to do what the Lord wanted me to do and had prepared me for," Miss Lucy recalled, "but I wondered if I were really ready for what was there. It was something new. There had never been a secretary for the Orient before, and I was going out to be his associate. That gave me an unusual feeling as I thought about it. It scared and excited me, yet I did wonder.

"Then there was the realization that I was leaving home, and my loved ones would be ten thousand miles away. I knew it would be seven years before I would see them again."

Soon after Lucy arrived in China, the Foreign Mission Board changed the time to five years between furloughs, but she did not know that when she started out across the Pacific, nor did her family.

Family and friends went to the train to see her off. There were hugs, loving advice, and gifts showered upon her as she boarded the train for Seattle, Washington. The Young Woman's Auxiliary members gave her a copy of the current best seller *Gone with the Wind* so that she could agonize over Scarlet's problems instead of her own while crossing the ocean.

Miss Lucy arrived in Seattle on schedule. She met three other missionaries who were going over on the same ship.

She had been told she didn't need a visa to enter China. But upon her arrival in Seattle on Friday afternoon, she discovered that a visa was required. By the time she had checked into her hotel, everything was closed, and nothing could be done about getting a visa until morning.

The ship was leaving shortly after lunch, giving Lucy the entire morning to get her visa. She and the other missionaries thought she had plenty of time.

Saturday morning she went to the Chinese embassy. When she arrived the embassy was closed, and all the gates were locked and barred. She knocked and called until finally someone came. The man didn't speak much English, and she spoke no Chinese. She did manage to tell him what she needed.

He responded, "I'm sorry. We are closed." She explained she had to get the visa. She was leaving on the 1:30 ship.

He stalled for a while. Miss Lucy pleaded, and he repeated he could do nothing. After some agonizing minutes went by, they found a man who did speak English fluently. Again she explained who she was and the reason for her immediate need. He explained, "This is China's Double Tenth. Everything is closed."

"What shall I do?" Miss Lucy questioned. "I have to leave on that ship at 1:30 to go to Shanghai."

"The University of Shanghai?" the second man asked quickly.

She said she would not be teaching there but would be working in connection with the university.

"I'm a graduate of that university," he said. "If you are going there, you should have a visa. Just wait here, and I will see what I can do."

He returned later and said, "Keep waiting. There must be

some way." After the third time, he came in and handed her a visa.

Her companions had taken her baggage to the ship, the *President Jackson,* and were anxiously awaiting her arrival. They were delighted when she jumped out of the taxi, waving the precious visa.

"The ship looked enormous to me," Lucy said. "There were programs planned for our entertainment, with many interesting things to do. We enjoyed reading the books which friends had given to me. We talked about Chinese customs, and I asked many questions of the other missionaries, who were returning for another tour of duty."

As Miss Lucy recalled her first crossing of the Pacific, she said, "The first night out, we were right in the middle of a storm. My chair fell over, and I fell, but I wasn't hurt. The storm did not abate for several days. Instead of being frightened, I enjoyed it. All my life, I wanted to walk on water. At night I would stand out on the deck and look out on those deep green waves. I could see them rolling. The lights of the ship made the white caps look even brighter. I thought, *Oh, if I could only get out there and roll along with them.*"

A young Filipino joined Lucy one evening, as she was looking out at the water. They talked for some time, and Lucy asked, "Are you a Christian?"

He quickly answered, "Yes, I was born a Christian."

Sadly, she realized this young man was one of many who did not realize that one is not born a Christian but reborn through faith in Jesus Christ.

One night during the storm, she ate dinner with one of the officers. She asked if they were in any real danger. He said, "No, we are right in the center of the typhoon. As long as we stay in the center, we are safe." *This is so like life,* thought

Lucy. *In the center of God's will, we are safe.*

Lucy wrote a letter on October 20, 1936 to Dr. Maddry, executive secretary of the Foreign Mission Board, while she was on board the *President Jackson*. Part of the letter follows:

> "I sometimes find myself wondering if I am dreaming or if I really am on my way to China. I am very happy though and see more and more of the magnitude and importance of my task as I have time to think about it and study the needs. My constant prayer is that I may ever be ready for the task at hand and give my best to it. I have only one purpose on the field and that is to help others know our Lord. Anything that I can do which will do this is my task, and it is my joy and privilege.
>
> "I am sure the Lord has had a hand in our plans, and I am here because he made it plain to me that this was where he wanted me. Thus far his will has been plain and he has led me. I am sure he will continue to lead, so I go on without fear, trusting in his promises. I am looking forward to many happy years of service in the Orient and trust that I may ever give my best."

The *President Jackson* docked safely in Yokohama, Japan, her first port of call in Japan. Some missionaries met their ship. They took the new missionaries into town for one day of sight-seeing.

The next port was the beautiful hillside city of Kobe. They left the harbor at night. The lights of the city were brilliant as the ship pulled away from shore.

Four Japanese ships were in the harbor as the *President Jackson* left. They saluted the American ship by ringing their bells and waving to them as they passed by.

From Kobe, the ship sailed up the inland sea, instead of

going out into the ocean. The passengers were warned not to make any unusual noises, take pictures, or do anything that might be considered suspicious. The fact that they were Americans going into China caused the Japanese to watch them carefully.

The ship arrived in Shanghai a few days later. It was after dark, so the passengers remained on board until morning. Missionaries who lived in Shanghai welcomed the new missionaries royally.

Dr. Sampey, president of The Southern Baptist Theological Seminary, Louisville, Kentucky, and his wife were visiting in Shanghai. They invited Lucy to shop with them. She went along; but knowing very little about the value of Chinese money, she decided to wait before doing any shopping.

Lucy's introduction to the people of China was a delightful experience with a baby and his young mother. While she and the driver were sitting in the car waiting for the Sampeys to make one last stop, a young lady walked by. She was fascinated not only with the car but also with the foreigner in the car. She approached the car rather curiously. Lucy rolled down her window and held her arms out to the baby. Seeing Lucy's smile, the baby reached out to her without hesitation. She held him in her arms, as he explored her facial features and then turned to look around the car. The mother beamed her approval, but the driver was surprised that the baby would go so readily to a foreigner. She reminded him, "To children, there are no racial differences."

4
First Years in China

Arrangements had been made for Miss Lucy to live in a home with Misses Willy Kelley and Pearl Johnson. Miss Kelley had been in China for more than forty years. She was eighty-four years old when Miss Lucy arrived in China. Miss Johnson was younger. Both of them were a great help in making Miss Lucy's transition easier.

Miss Kelley had many friends among the Chinese and Americans. Some friends had given her two large two-story houses. They were large enough to accommodate the many missionaries and other guests. There were few, if any, hotels available in those days. As the missionaries came through Shanghai on their way to or from their fields of service, they spent time with Misses Kelley and Johnson. The large dining room had a table that could easily seat twenty-four. Later, during the war, many missionaries had to stay in one of these houses while awaiting passage out of China. At Miss Kelley's death, the houses became the property of the Foreign Mission Board.

Miss Kelley and the Chinese people had a mutual love and respect for one another. She spoke their language fluently. She worked at North Gate Church.

Miss Lucy also worked at North Gate Church, in addition to her work in the office. Since the people of the Shanghai area spoke the Wu language, that was the language Lucy learned first. She later studied Mandarin, the official language of China.

One of Miss Lucy's first invitations was to a luncheon, celebrating Shanghai University's anniversary. Miss Kelley worried about Miss Lucy's frail appetite, knowing how much food the Chinese served. Miss Kelley said that it would be all right to leave some of the food if Miss Lucy were sitting with other Americans. If she were sitting with Chinese, however, she would have to eat it. Miss Kelley really worried when she learned Miss Lucy was invited to a dinner in someone's home that same evening.

The day arrived. At the luncheon, Miss Lucy was invited to sit next to the wife of the president of the university. She enjoyed everything that was served. Miss Kelley was surprised when Miss Lucy returned home looking well but cautioned her she would have to eat again that evening.

At the dinner, Miss Lucy, as one of the new missionaries, was seated with the guests of honor. Tea and hors d'oeuvres were served, followed by ten or twelve courses.

After the meal, everyone went to another room for fruit. Miss Lucy had no ill effects and loved the foods.

The Chinese enjoyed holidays to the fullest. The Chinese New Year was a very important holiday. The Christians celebrated the occasion with a church service. After the worship service, they had a program where individuals, as well as groups, participated. Miss Lucy attended one of the New Year celebrations. There were songs, speeches, pantomines, and skits. All ages took part. One woman left her seat, talking as she made her way to the platform. The people in front were laughing, so Miss Lucy strained to hear what was being said. The woman said, "For a year now I've listened to Mandarin. You know it's not my language. I'm from Shanghai. Now you listen to me." Even those who could not understand the woman seemed to enjoy listening as she spoke. In one meeting Miss Lucy attended, five different languages were spoken. It was amusing but confusing even with interpreters.

In a letter to Miss Ford at the Foreign Mission Board, Miss Lucy wrote, "I think that which impresses me most of all is the people. Everywhere you turn, there are people, not just a few, but throngs of them, and so few know anything about our Lord."

Offices were prepared for Lucy and Dr. Rankin in the True Light Building. This building was owned jointly by Southern Baptist and a General Missions group. The treasurer of the Baptist work in the Orient had an office there. After Miss Lucy's arrival, the necessary changes were made for her to have an office too. All of the offices were on the seventh floor. The Baptist Book Store occupied the lower floor.

The work in China was already established. The Sunday School and young people's work were well organized. The only new part was having a secretary and his associate to coordinate all of the Southern Baptist work in China. Because of the wide expanse of China, each of the mission stations worked almost independently of the other missionaries.

Both Dr. Rankin and Miss Lucy were aware that many of the missionaries had been in China for a long time. None of them knew exactly what to expect from the new program. They wondered what changes, if any, would be made. If the establishment of the regional office for the Orient were not handled with love and in the common interest for all, the office could cause resentment.

There were five missions in China: North China, South China, Central China, Interior China, and Manchuria. Each had its own organization.

The work had begun originally in South China, but

First Years in China

Manchuria and North China were so far away, it was difficult to coordinate the work. Some airplanes were operating on scheduled flights, and train service had shown a marked improvement. With hope for better transportation facilities and communication, Dr. Rankin and Miss Lucy started making plans to make possible all of them working together.

The harmonious manner in which Dr. Rankin and Miss Lucy were able to get 250 missionaries to make plans together for the future and work together in love speaks well for their ability.

Within a few months after Miss Lucy's arrival, they held the first joint young people's meeting. The meeting was held in Hwang Shien, where a Baptist seminary and hospital were located. Weeks of planning preceded the event. Young people from all over China were there. Chinese homes and missionary homes were opened to the students. Miss Lucy was one of the missionaries who participated in the activities. She didn't understand a great deal that was said because her knowledge of the language was still rather limited. The different dialects spoken by the students made interpreters necessary. But everyone enjoyed the beautiful spirit of the people who attended.

One night during the meeting, a young doctor who was taking some seminary work stood. He said, "God has called me to preach. I want to go out into West China where there is no church and no hospital."

His wife added, "The Lord has been dealing with me too. I am ready to go with him."

During the week of the conference, a nurse, a kindergarten teacher, and a Bible woman—one who was trained to visit and teach women in their homes—said they were ready to go with the young doctor and his family.

Money was needed for all of their needs and transportation. The young people said, "We will get the money. We will send them." Each organization agreed to give what they could. They appointed Miss Lucy to be in charge of the money.

She accepted the job. Later, recalling the event, Miss Lucy said, "In the next few weeks, the letters started coming. The letters held money. It was hard to hold back the tears. Sometimes it would be so torn and so dirty, I knew it was a real sacrifice."

The next day, before the young people returned to their homes, the Sino-Japanese war started. The Japanese started their offensive in the North. The things some of them encountered en route to their homes were unbelievable.

Miss Lucy and Dr. and Mrs. Rankin went from the meeting to Peking. They did not know the war had started. Dr. Rankin went to Peita Ho and met some new missionaries who had just come to the language school. The women planned some sight-seeing and shopping in Peking while he was away.

Miss Lucy and Mrs. Rankin had never been to Peking before, so they got up early the next morning to see the city. Completely unaware of their danger, they went to see the Forbidden City, the Summer Palace, the Marble Boat, and the Ming Tombs. Little Mary Lee Rankin, who was with the women, was beginning to tire of the sight-seeing until they got to the room of the clocks in the Summer Palace. There were more than a thousand clocks in the room. She was totally fascinated as she watched the movements of all those clocks. The clocks were all sizes and shapes.

The Japanese started bombing Peking that night. Many of the buildings were destroyed. That was Miss Lucy's last trip to Peking.

First Years in China

Dr. Rankin did not know the war had started when he left Peita Ho for Peking at the end of the week. Although he spoke Cantonese fluently, the people in that area of China spoke Mandarin. He had to change trains at Tientsin. The conductor came in and said, "If you are going to Peking, stay where you are. We'll take this coach on." Normally, they walked several blocks to another station.

Dr. Rankin met a well-dressed, nice-looking man on his coach. In China, the seats on the train face each other. When he saw the man, Dr. Rankin thought, *Now I should be able to speak Mandarin so I could communicate with him.* While he was concentrating on the language, the man sat down facing him and said, "How are you?"

"*Wapitang,*" Dr. Rankin said in Cantonese. Then he realized that the man had spoken to him in English. He laughed, and the other man joined him.

When the train stopped in Peking, Dr. Rankin got off and started looking for a ricksha to take him out to the hotel where his family and Miss Lucy were staying. None of the drivers wanted to take him. He still didn't know about the war and couldn't understand why they refused. He finally bargained with one man who agreed to take him.

The Rankin family and Miss Lucy had train reservations to leave Peking, but they were canceled. They were able, however, to leave Peking on a later train on Sunday afternoon. The station was crowded. A mass of milling people looked worried and unsure. Two American tour groups who had been in Peking all week were at the station. Their tour guide was afraid for them to leave the hotel, so they had not seen Peking. How fortunate for Mrs. Rankin and Miss Lucy that they had had no tour guide to keep them from seeing the city. They bought peanut butter, cheese, and crackers in case the train was delayed. It did take two days for the trip, and they were grateful for the extra food they had taken.

Peaches were in season, and vendors were at each station stop. All of the passengers bought peaches to supplement their food. They carried little compacts filled with disinfectant and cotton when they traveled. One of the teachers on the train bought peaches for her group and was carefully wiping each peach with the disinfectant. She only had one small piece of cotton, which she used until it was so dirty it hardly helped. Fortunately, the people peeled the peaches before eating them.

After her return to Shanghai, Miss Lucy received a letter from the young doctor in Hwang Shien saying they were ready to go. Some money had been allocated for equipment for the hospital, but there was not enough money for all five volunteers to go. She wrote a letter explaining there was only enough money for two of them.

Miss Lucy met the ship on which the two volunteers were traveling to Shanghai. She wondered which of them would be on the ship. The doctor and nurse stepped off. Miss Lucy started asking questions.

The doctor said, "When your letter came, I took it over to Dr. Culpepper, a teacher in the seminary. He called all five of us together. Everyone agreed that I should go. My wife rose with the two children and said, 'I won't use the money. We will walk and meet him in West China sometime next summer.'

"The little Bible woman said, 'They will need me later; I will walk with her.'

"The kindergarten teacher added, 'She will need help with the children, so I will go with them.'" And that was how

First Years in China

they decided that the doctor and the nurse were to go to West China.

Miss Lucy asked what route the others were taking. When the doctor answered, Miss Lucy said, "Oh, they can't go that way. The Japanese have just started a big offensive there."

The doctor dropped his eyes; but, like the others, he knew it was impossible to reach the travelers. He said, "We'll just have to hold them up to the Lord."

The doctor and nurse stayed in Shanghai long enough to get the equipment they needed and left by plane, not knowing when they would arrive in West China.

Weeks went by. One evening in a little village in West China, a woman sat by the bedside of her sick child. As she tried to soothe the feverish child, she said, "Oh, if your daddy were only here he would know what to do for you. I don't know anything else to do."

That same evening a lonely man walked down the street. He was far from home and concerned about his family. As he walked along praying and wondering what to do, he heard a baby cry. He stopped and listened: *That's my baby. It can't be, but I know it is.* He walked in the direction of the cries. He knocked on the door, and there were his wife and their children and the other two volunteers. He did know what to do for the baby. At that joyous moment, the doctor, his wife and children, the kindergarten teacher, the nurse, and the Bible woman were reunited through God's care.

5
Interrupted by War

Shanghai was calmer than Peking, and Miss Lucy and Dr. Rankin went on with their regular schedule for two weeks. There were groups of soldiers around, but there was no fighting. Miss Lucy and Lorene Tilford, a missionary appointed at the same time Miss Lucy was, were going up to Kuling for language study. The language school was on top of a beautiful mountain. They walked part of the way and were carried in chairs by coolies to the top. Everything was conducive for learning.

Even in the north, the fighting had stopped temporarily, and in Shanghai area there was nothing. After two weeks, the fighting resumed, and bombs started falling in Shanghai. For several weeks the missionaries were stranded in Kuling. Miss Lucy worried about all the things she should be doing in Shanghai, but there was nothing she could do to change the situation. She wrote to Miss Ford:

> "While it has been cool and comfortable up here, it has not been as quiet and peaceful as we should have liked for it to have been on account of the conditions elsewhere in China. For more than a month now, we have been living one day at a time wondering just what to do. One day it would look as if we should make our plans to stay here for the winter, and the next it would look as if we

Interrupted by War 37

should leave here as soon as possible. About three weeks ago the Consul sent us word that Kuling was safe and the Japanese had promised not to disturb it, so we could stay here in safety, until conditions settled in Shanghai for us to return there. A week ago yesterday, however, the Consul from Hankow came up here to meet with the Americans and told us that the Embassy had reason to believe that Kuling would no longer be a safe place to be, especially for those whose work was near the coast or the north, so advised all who could possibly leave should make arrangements as soon as possible. They say that it would surprise no one if the Japanese were to bomb the Hankow-Canton Railway most any time. If that should happen we would be here with no way to get out, for it is already impossible to return to Shanghai via Nanking or Hungchow."

She concluded the letter by writing, "We can get a blessing out of every experience if we try."

The Southern Baptists on the mountain got together to decide what to do. The consul suggested that those who had furloughs due in the near future should return to America. If Miss Lucy had been in Shanghai when the bombing started, she would have had to go to Manila with the other missionaries.

Miss Tilford and Miss Lucy were able to get a train into Canton. The route through Woose into Canton was a beautiful ride. For three days they traveled with mountains on one side and the clear water of the river on the other. Lush green vegetables grew in gardens along the track.

The missionaries rode third class on a third class train. There was no air conditioning on the train, so it was extremely hot. They sat on boards and were given a sheet so they could sleep on those boards at night. They spent most of the time standing out in the vestibule where it was cooler. They were delighted to learn that their language teachers were on the same train. The trip became more interesting as they pointed out things along the way and so studied the language as they traveled.

Miss Tilford and Miss Lucy arrived in Canton one morning, hoping to rest before resuming their trip. To their dismay, a cook was preparing breakfast so passengers could eat hurriedly and get the next train into Hong Kong.

There was fighting in the area, so the train rushed through as quickly as possible to Hong Kong. The missionaries then went to an island. A typhoon had swept the island just three days earlier. Miss Lucy and Miss Tilford were shocked by the devastation. But missionaries living there offered a place for them to stay.

Miss Tilford was studying Cantonese, so she stayed on the island for study. But Miss Lucy was anxious to get back to Shanghai. She boarded a French gunboat and arrived in Shanghai a few days later.

The havoc which she found in Shanghai was a far cry from what she had left a short time before. Most of the buildings were boarded up, but many shop doors carried signs saying, "Business as Usual." With the majority of the small shop owners, the money they made on any given day was the only money they had. "Neither Chinese nor missionaries are letting these things keep them from their work. Every effort possible is being made to care for the physical needs of the people, and then our Christians are busy preaching and teaching. The Lord has been good to us. None of our folk has been injured," Miss Lucy wrote home.

Interrupted by War 39

The women and children had been evacuated after the bombing of Shanghai on August 13, but the men were trying to carry on the work. The situation was very tense. Fighting was raging throughout the area, and no one knew what to expect. Some of the women returned, and some of them even went back to the schools or churches in which they had been working.

During all of this, the missionaries watched the progress of the war very carefully, knowing the United States would probably be involved. Sometimes the United States Government would ask Dr. Rankin and Miss Lucy to check on missionaries in areas considered to be dangerous. They kept in close contact with the Foreign Mission Board office in Richmond. The situation became more intense, and they had no choice but to send the mothers and children home. When the United States ordered women and children to leave China, the next decision was whether the men should accompany them.

Miss Lucy said, "November 20, 1940, will stand out in my mind as long as I live, as we saw mothers and children board that ship, leaving daddies behind. 'Goodbye, Daddy' will ring in my ears forever."

They left the day before Thanksgiving Day. Miss Lucy had heard some of the wives express concern about their husbands being alone on that special day. But in spite of the uneasy circumstances, the servants cooked a Thanksgiving dinner for the missionaries who remained in Shanghai.

Miss Lucy recalled that time in China. "Some of the tragedies of having to leave China were missionaries like Miss Annie Hartwell, who had spent all but eleven of her seventy-seven years in China. Her parents had been missionaries, and she had served in that capacity for many years. She had gone with no intentions of ever going back to America to live. She planned to spend her life there and to die with her beloved Chinese.

"When the government ordered the evacuation, there were so many Americans in China, including other missions as well as our own, they chartered a ship to take them. Our missionaries had to come to Shanghai to board the ship. Since some of them had to leave when they could get transportation to Shanghai, many of them spent several days with us. We rented cots or any kinds of beds we could get.

"I couldn't see putting that seventy-seven-year-old lady on a cot to sleep, so I gave her my bed, and I slept on the cot. It was a joy to have her there with us. She had many interesting tales to tell. She had us laughing one minute and in tears the next.

"Miss Annie never took a nap. She was always busy doing something. The other women took time to rest in the afternoon. One day while everyone else was asleep, a man came to the door. He said he was collecting antiques and asked if they had any. She said, 'Yes, we have lots of them.' He asked if he could come in and see them. She said, 'Oh no, they are all asleep.'

"On the day the ship sailed, we were extremely busy getting everyone off. There are always last minute changes to be reckoned with. We stayed there until the ship left. It was late when I got home and much later when I went to my room. Under my pillow I found a paper. Miss Annie had written, 'I hope you will excuse the tear drops on this note. I have tried many times to write to tell how much I appreciate your giving me your room and your bed, giving me a place to rest. I'm leaving China which is home to me. I don't know what I'll do, but the Lord has led this far, and I am sure he will continue to lead. Goodbye, darling, and thanks for everything.'

"The next day we talked about her and other older missionaries who were leaving what they felt was home. Some of the other groups lacked the planning that our missionaries had for their evacuation. How grateful we were for our Foreign Mission Board. Their love, concern, and compassion for our missionaries who had gone out to serve the Lord was a constant blessing to us."

The Japanese remained on the far side of the river, sending shells into Shanghai. The shells fell all around the compound. They were firing right over the roofs of the two houses where the missionaries lived. Miss Lucy worked at the office, keeping the telephone busy checking on other missionaries. In spite of the closeness of the firing, no one in the mission compound was hurt, nor were any of the buildings damaged.

The Japanese had annihilated one little village just outside Shanghai. The survivors were placed in a refugee camp. The Chinese could not travel outside the city alone, but Miss Lucy was allowed to take five of them at a time with her. They went through the north gate of the city and walked to the refugee camp every Sunday afternoon for worship services. One afternoon one of the guards asked for her pass. He saw that she was a United States citizen. He asked what state she was from. She answered, "Oklahoma." Whether there was magic in that word or he was just curious she didn't know, but he did let them go on.

Miss Lucy wrote a letter to Dr. Maddry on February 9, 1939:

"If it were not for the fairer side of the picture, I fear most folk could not remain in China, but there is a brighter side. Our hearts leap with joy and our tongues praise the Lord for all the many wonderful blessings that we have. Truly he has blessed and is continuing to bless the efforts of his children and the Kingdom work goes on in spite of all the attempts to block the progress. Some of us were saying yesterday, that as awful as this experience has been for everyone, there were some who had received such blessings as they would not exchange for anything. Christians, Chinese and missionaries have surely proven their faith during these past two years.

"I am still enjoying the work and am not sorry I made the decision to come here.

"For one who has had a definite mission call and loves to work with other races who do not know the Lord, now is the time to be in China."

Other letters indicate the pleasure Miss Lucy had in her work in spite of the war. October 10, 1939, her letter to Miss Ford said, "Money has become a problem. One day Shanghai checks are at a premium, then again the folks can't use them at all. We can't buy Federal Reserve notes in Shanghai. Many places can't sell drafts or checks. Conditions change so fast, we let each day take care of itself."

A letter to Miss Ford on May 13, 1940, indicated that the work was going well. "We had a good mission meeting. There was a fine spirit. Everyone was encouraged from the reports and the future of our work. Now there are many wonderful opportunities and souls are being saved."

That same day, a letter to Dr. Maddry said, "The Lord is blessing the efforts of his people and his kingdom is going forward in China. There is much more we could do if we had more people and more time."

Interrupted by War

A letter written on July 15 to Dr. Maddry said, "General conditions in the Orient are about as unsettled as they have been for the last three years, but we rejoice in the wonderful way the Lord has blessed his work and workers through all the days and conditions. We find so much for which to thank Him and so much to encourage and strengthen our faith. Souls are being saved every day."

In the beginning, only the missionary women and children were evacuated from North China. But as the fighting got worse, all of the missionaries had to leave. Arrangements for temporary housing had to be made for them until they could get transportation back to the United States. Elizabeth Ward who stayed in China was interned in prison camp.

February 25, 1941, Miss Lucy wrote to Dr. Maddry:

"Our work goes on in a wonderful way, no matter what happens. We rejoice in what the Lord is doing through His people here in the Orient. We continue to hope and pray that our missionaries will not all have to leave China, but if we do, Kingdom work will go on and souls will be saved. Some of the Lord's elect are here and they will be true no matter what experiences come their way. The devotion and consecration of the missionaries and the Chinese co-workers will ever be a challenge and inspiration to those who have been with them and know of what they are going through these days.

"According to present plans, I'll be coming home this summer for furlough. I am having a hard time convincing myself that it is the thing to do, and I'm not quite sure even yet. When there is so much to be done and so few to do it and no hope of getting others here to give it a lift, it seems very unwise for those of us who are here to leave if we can stay on. I am making my plans to go when the time comes but am prepared to stay on longer if it seems wise. These are days when we are constantly praying for wisdom to know what to do from day to day."

In response to that letter, Dr. Maddry wrote, "Dr. Rankin has written me several times about the wonderful work you are doing. He spoke in highest terms of your work and does not know what he will do when you come. I am glad indeed that you have been able to be in China in this great epoch-making hour."

After much prayer and consideration, Dr. Rankin and Miss Lucy decided it was best for her to take her furlough when it was due.

Miss Lucy had been in China the five years required to have a furlough. They decided she should leave as soon as she could book passage home. She arrived in the United States two months before the Japanese attack on Pearl Harbor.

One of the first things Miss Lucy did when she got home was to make a big batch of candy to send to the remaining staff in China. Then came the attack on Pearl Harbor. She was in Richmond several months later when a package came for her. She recognized it at once. The candy she had sent to China had been forwarded to her in Richmond. It was still good, so the people there enjoyed it.

On January 1, 1942, Dr. Maddry asked Miss Lucy to report to Richmond. She planned to work in the Foreign Mission Board office. In April of that year, she had to have spinal fusion surgery. She was in a cast for six months, which curtailed her activity somewhat. After the six months, she returned to Oklahoma City from which she traveled for the time she remained in the United States. She traveled for the

Interrupted by War

Board wherever she needed to go. Her traveling was done by bus or train.

Shortly after the war ended, Miss Lucy received a wire from the Foreign Mission Board. It said, "Cancel all plans, and wait for letter."

So she waited but she did not stop her scheduled activities. She had been invited out to dinner with friends one Friday evening. Just as they were leaving, she received a wire saying, "Come to New York in one week."

Miss Lucy had many arrangements to make to get ready to return to China. She had to check on her visa, get the necessary shots, pack, and do all necessary shopping. The Foreign Mission Board called from Richmond to tell her not to worry if that was not enough time, they could delay her departure. But Miss Lucy was anxious to return to China and did not want to delay.

A friend offered to help Effie Katherine, who was helping Lucy pack. Exactly one week later, Miss Lucy boarded the train for New York City. She arrived the next day and left for China on Sunday.

6
Communists in China

When World War II was over, the missionaries began to return to China. The problem of rebuilding was monumental. The homes of missionaries, as well as homes of the Chinese, had to be repaired or rebuilt. Many of the schools, hospitals, and churches had been completely demolished. The house Miss Kelley lived in had not been destroyed because the Japanese had needed some spacious grounds for their use. The China Inland Mission had a big compound where they had a school, hospital, and other facilities. The Japanese had taken that compound for their use during the war. The China Inland Mission had moved the missionaries into the two houses belonging to Miss Kelley. The houses were crowded, but the missionaries did their best to protect and look after the property.

When Miss Lucy returned to Shanghai on January 2, 1946, her home was at least partially ready for occupancy. The servants there were ready to help. Her first week was busy but very rewarding. A letter to Dr. Rankin told of her joy of being back in China. "For twelve happy days I have been in Shanghai. There is so much to do, it is hard to know what to do first. The future is more promising and more thrilling than the past, so great days are ahead for us. There are problems, of course, but these can be met with the same faith and courage as in the past."

Communists in China 47

After a short time, enough of the buildings were repaired to provide housing for the returning missionaries, who were anxious to get back to doing what God had called them to do. Miss Lucy said of that time, "We began again. The Lord still lives, and the work will go on. He was there to show us what needed to be done and how to do it. The Lord was good to us in those days when we so desperately needed him."

Miss Elizabeth Ward, who had been released from her internment by the Japanese, had gone to the offices to straighten them. Dr. Baker James Cauthen had replaced Dr. Rankin as the area secretary. Dr. Rankin was the new executive secretary of the Foreign Mission Board.

Two groups, each made up of a national pastor and deacon and a missionary, went up country to check on the work, find what damage had been done, and how long it would be before the women and children could return.

Because the rebuilding and repairing of the buildings took time, Dr. Cauthen asked the Foreign Mission Board to send only one ship of returning missionaries at a time. The Board complied with this request, but they did not figure on a shipping strike. The strike caused some of the ships to be held up for a time and then released with others headed for the Orient. Consequently, three ships arrived in Shanghai on the same day.

Miss Lucy scoured the area for all the beds she could find and started setting them up all over the house. One of the little "missionary kids" went down to the dock with Miss Lucy to meet a group of returning missionaries. Miss Lucy was the only one who could go on board the ship. She would go on board, bring off one or two babies, hand them to someone waiting at the dock, then go back after more. The little boy watched for a while, then he said, "Aunt Lucy, where are all of these people going to sleep?"

She said, "Well, we'll just wait until the first bunch goes to sleep, then we'll just roll them out on the floor and let the next group go to bed."

He looked rather serious for a moment, and then said, "Aw, Aunt Lucy, you wouldn't do that, would you?"

Christmas is always exciting, but with all of those people in two houses, it was truly an experience that year. Snow covered the ground, which was unusual, but it added to the Christmas feeling. The Chinese had a beautiful worship service at the church on Christmas Eve.

The missionairies were so excited and happy to be back in China that many of them had difficulty thinking of sleep. About the time they had started to retire, they heard the Chinese Christians out on the lawn, singing Christmas carols. They invited them in, served hot chocolate, and had a wonderful time of fellowship and rejoicing. It was a Christmas long to be remembered.

Food was scarce, but the US Army surplus food was released in 1946, and they could buy American canned goods at reasonable prices. Before the war, the missionaries had lived on native foods. Now they supplemented the American canned foods with local vegetables. The canned foods the missionaries kept for themselves were those which the Chinese wouldn't eat because of their different tastes.

In a letter to Dr. Rankin, dated January 7, 1947, Miss Lucy expressed her usual optimism:

> "Evangelistic opportunities this fall and winter have been many and the results most encouraging. Last Sunday Dr. McMillan baptized forty-two at North Gate. That is the third time since spring we have had baptismal services

and each of the other two times there have been more than thirty baptisms. We have another group awaiting the next service. Other churches and schools have had the same experience. We had an interesting thing happen last night. The others had all gone to their rooms, most of them to bed, when I heard someone step up on the porch. I called down to see who it was and what he wanted. He asked for Dr. McMillan, but when told he was not here, he produced a note to Pearl and me from Dr. McMillan, asking that we talk to him should he come by to see us. He had met him on the train several days ago and talked to him about being a Christian. Although it was raining hard and the wind was cold and raw as it could be, he had gone out to hear the gospel. Dr. Harris was here and talked to him quite a long time. The man went away very impressed and said he really wanted to know more and would be back. He seemed to really be in earnest and wanted to have that peace for which he said he had been looking a long time. It is not at all unusual for people to come to some of us asking to know the way of life."

There were many happy times. One missionary had a surprise party on his sixty-fifth birthday. He received a jade charm with the Chinese character for happiness on it for his watch chain.

A typhoon in June kept the missionaries in Shanghai mopping water which blew in through the windows, but there was no other damage to their property.

Miss Lucy wrote to Dr. Rankin on July 15, 1948, concerning the Communist buildup in China.

"This morning the papers carried the news that

Yenchow had fallen and so is now in the hands of the Communists. Just what that means we do not know. We have kept in touch with the American Consul there. Mr. Wang sent us word last week not to worry if Yenchow fell, for he felt sure the Communists would not harm our folks. That helps some, but we do not know when their policy will change, so we are getting our folk out as soon as possible. The Catholics have more than a hundred folk in Yenchow whom they have been trying to get out. We have worked together a great deal on this and neither have been successful yet.

"Dr. Cauthen is in Naking today meeting the missionaries and Chinese co-workers from Honan. The fall of Kaifeng and the continued fighting in that area has caused many serious problems and some decisions had to be made as to what to do. We have been much in prayer the last few days for this meeting."

In spite of the growing strength of the Communists in China, the missionaries were able to carry on their work until 1949. By then some of the missionaries had to leave the areas in which they were working. All missionaries eventually were advised to return to Shanghai.

Although the missionaries tried to carry on their regular work, the difficulty of doing that is indicated in a letter Miss Lucy wrote to Mary Lib Fuqua October 10, 1949. "We are watching events carefully these days. The fall of Kukong makes the end of other places seem nearer, but we do not know what will happen."

About this time, Miss Lucy spent five days in the mountains of Taipei at a young people's conference. The young people were interested and eager to know about the Lord and

Communists in China 51

his work. Ten people made professions of faith in Christ. The consecration service in the church on Sunday night was a fitting climax to the retreat.

Back in Shanghai, Miss Lucy joined the staff of the Orient office in making plans for relocation if the Communists took over Shanghai. Missionaries in many places were trying to decide whether to stay. The hospital in Woochow was still open. Dr. Bill Wallace and Miss Everley Hayes were stationed there. Miss Hayes was evacuated because of the fighting. Dr. Cauthen and Miss Lucy went up there to see Dr. Wallace after Miss Hayes had gone.

Dr. Wallace said to them, "I'm just one man. No one is dependent on me. I have one sister, but she has a husband to care for her. I'll stay. If I get killed, it's all right."

Miss Lucy recalled her feelings from that day, "Dr. Cauthen and I went back to Hong Kong with heavy hearts, knowing that Dr. Wallace's decision to stay would probably mean his death. The Chinese people loved him and realized how much he loved them because he stayed." Dr. Wallace was imprisoned by the Communists when they captured Woochow. "Dr. Wallace was killed by the Communist guards. His death will long be remembered by the Chinese people and those of us who knew him. His death was not in vain."

In March, it was obvious the missionaries would have to leave China. Miss Lucy went to Hong Kong to find places for evacuating missionaries to live and to open offices for headquarters for the Orient. Finding a place was difficult. Her first inquiry was disappointing. She was told it was too late; every available building was taken. As Miss Lucy said, "The Lord always has a way to do what needs to be done." In visiting with some Chinese Christians, she learned that two Baptist deacons were with a company that was building a new apartment house. They agreed to let Miss Lucy set up headquarters there. It was a three-story house, and the company reserved only one apartment. This left adequate living space in the beginning, but as more people began to come in, it was necessary to find more housing. Those arrangements were made. As the missionaries came out of China, they had places to live and to work. Consequently, the work expanded to new fields.

Miss Lucy was the first Southern Baptist missionary to Hong Kong. A century earlier, Mr. and Mrs. J. L. Shuck had been assigned there by the Baptist Triennial Convention. As soon as Miss Lucy was able to establish an office in Hong Kong, the United States Government and the Foreign Mission Board called. Heavy fighting was reported in certain areas of China, and the missionaries in those places needed to be brought out. The staff of the new Orient office kept in close contact with the office in Richmond, both to give and receive information. Telephone service into China was very poor. Miss Lucy went to the telephone office in Hong Kong and explained how important it was for her to be able to reach her office in Shanghai. They suggested that 9:00 on Monday mornings would be the most likely time that she could get through. They reserved that time for her. She sent a cable to Dr. Cauthen and told him she would call on Monday mornings. For a while, she had access to that phone for fifteen minutes every Monday. This proved a blessing to the missionaries in China and to families in America who had not been able to contact their loved ones. One morning she let a businessman, who could not otherwise get through, use a few minutes of their time.

"It was wonderful how the Lord took care of us and always managed to put us where we needed to be," Miss Lucy concluded.

In addition to her work in the office, Miss Lucy taught a

Sunday School class for young people. She and her Sunday School class worked together to find housing for the Chinese Christians and missionaries who were arriving in Hong Kong from China.

Miss Lucy stayed in Hong Kong for a year before she went home on furlough. There were many things to do in preparing to leave. Things were very uncertain. Some of the missionaries who were evacuating from China were due furloughs, and some took early furloughs. Missions in different countries called the Orient office, asking for more workers in their areas. One such call was from Korea. After several calls and letters to the people in Korea as well as to the Board in Richmond, Dr. Cauthen spent a week in Korea. He told the people to consider everything that would be involved in Southern Baptist missionaries beginning work in Korea, pray about it, and then let the Orient office know their decision.

The Baptist work in Korea had been done by Canadian Baptists, started by Malcom Fenwick, and there were differences. A short time later, their convention voted to invite Southern Baptists into Korea, and John Abernathy went to start the work. When the Korean War started, they had to leave, but they returned, and Baptist work has continued in South Korea.

There was work to be done, new places to do it, and willing workers to go, so God's work continued without interruption. When the Communists finally took over China, Southern Baptist missionaries were already located in other parts of the Orient. Mission work was started in the Philippines, Korea, Pakistan, Okinawa, Malaysia, Taiwan, Thailand, Singapore, Indonesia, and other places where Chinese lived.

Dr. and Mrs. Charles Culpepper, missionaries in China for many years, returned from furlough to Hong Kong where they took over Miss Lucy's work when she went home. Then Dr. and Mrs. Connely who had served in North China came. Dr. Connely took over the treasurer's work, releasing Dr. Culpepper to work in the seminary.

Chinese friends decided to have the farewells and welcomes together, so Miss Lucy and the Culpeppers were royally entertained. One evening they were invited out to dinner. Miss Lucy said, "They really put the little pot in the big pot for that meal." It was northern Chinese cooking as opposed to Cantonese, which happened to be her favorite.

At Miss Lucy's final farewell party, some of the convention people brought a package, about three feet long and three feet wide. When she went through customs in San Francisco, she was asked what she was carrying. She said, "A Chinese ship."

A customs officer said, "I surely would like to see it, but I'm not going to ask you to open it here." She got home with it still packed as it was when they gave it to her. Edmund, her nephew, put it together. It was a beautiful work of art. She later gave it to Oklahoma Baptist University.

On the day of her departure, she left again with mixed emotions. Knowing that she would probably return to Japan instead of Hong Kong, she went through Japan on her way back to the United States.

After four busy years in China and one in Hong Kong, Miss Lucy left for home in December, 1950.

In a letter to Dr. Cauthen from her home in Oklahoma City, Miss Lucy said, "I can never thank God enough or doubt his leadership for a moment when I look back over how he has worked and what he has done for us in the Orient in the last five years."

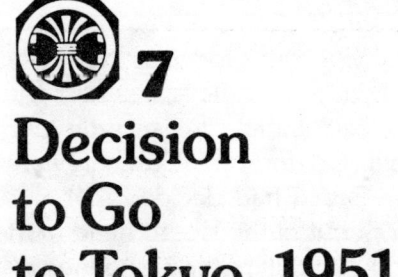

7
Decision to Go to Tokyo, 1951

While Miss Lucy was in Oklahoma City on furlough, she received a letter from Dr. Cauthen, concerning her going to Tokyo when she left America:

> "This letter is to set before you the question of your going to Tokyo. Even before the plans were definite for the location of my office in Tokyo I had been feeling that your presence there would be of very great value because of the strength you could bring to the treasurer's office.
>
> "Even during the few days you stopped in Tokyo on your way home you made a definite contribution to the mission. . . . your serving in connection with the Japan treasurer's office would be a most strategic contribution.
>
> "This would not mean that you are burning all of the bridges between you and China. If and when the door opens to go back to Shanghai I would certainly anticipate your return to the office there to take up just where we left off. It would be wonderful if we could see our headquarters office established in the True Light Building again, but it may be some time before that is a possibility. You would not need to feel, therefore, that your going to Japan now would mean not getting back to China when the way opens."

For the rest of her furlough, Miss Lucy prayed and thought about her future in the Orient.

She felt God was calling her to Japan, so she went to Tokyo in 1951. This was Miss Lucy's first experience living on the field without the secretary for the Orient also living on the field. Dr. and Mrs. Cauthen were living in Richmond because the Board had decided that all of the area secretaries would work out of the Board headquarters.

The culture and language of Japan was naturally different from what Miss Lucy was used to in China. But she found the Japanese as easy to love as her Chinese friends had been. In fact, a number of Chinese lived in Tokyo. She saw many things that reminded her of China, including Chinese restaurants which she enjoyed.

Miss Lucy went to Tokyo to assist Mr. Edwin Dozier, treasurer for the Japan Mission. The Dozier family had been in Japan for many years. They had won the love and respect of the Japanese people. Mother Dozier, as Edwin's mother was called, returned to Japan after the war and had a strong, steadying influence on the work.

The Japanese Convention wanted to evangelize all of Japan. They sent a request to the Foreign Mission Board, "If we put a Japanese couple to work in each church, will you place a missionary there?" The Board agreed.

Where possible churches were staffed by Japanese pastors. When there were more Japanese churches than missionary couples, single women were sent. The missionaries were very capable and assisted the Japanese pastors in establishing the church programs. At first, the Japanese had a difficult time appreciating the single women's abilities. They were not accustomed to women working in their churches. A short time later though, some of the Japanese pastors asked Miss Lucy for "Miss Missionaries."

Dr. Connely, Mr. Dozier, or Miss Lucy visited the new

Decision to Go to Tokyo, 1951

areas where mission work was being started. Sometimes new missionaries began work on the field before they were able to speak the language. When that happened, the missionaries worked through interpreters. Part of Miss Lucy's traveling duties was looking after missionaries who were ill. When necessary, she made arrangements to have the missionaries taken to Tokyo where the best hospital facilities were available.

Most of the work previously had been done in Kyushu in southern Japan. The Japanese Convention voted to establish headquarters in Tokyo. Finding places for churches and homes for the missionaries was not easy because the war had completely ravaged Japan. There was little equipment to work with, and food was scarce.

Some portable housing was used for churches and homes. One Japanese home was purchased that had been finished just before the war started but had never been lived in and was not damaged. Later they bought a building from the Buddhists to use for headquarters. Both office space and parking were available. The parking space was not as important then as it would be today. At that time there were few Japanese cars. Most of the cars in Tokyo were American made and imported by business and military people. If a Japanese owned a car, he probably bought it from a military person who was leaving for home.

Soon after Miss Lucy arrived in Japan, Dr. and Mrs. Frank Connely came from Hong Kong. He had been the treasurer there and took that position in Japan.

A letter was sent to the National City Bank of New York and Tokyo certifying that Frank H. Connely, treasurer of the Japan Mission of the Foreign Mission Board of the Southern Baptist Convention, had the authority to authorize Miss Lucy E. Smith, assistant treasurer of the Japan Mission, to sign checks on the local account. The financial part of Miss Lucy's job was established.

By September, 1952, their houses were finished and they were ready to settle down for the winter. Miss Lucy lived in a prefabricated house at first. In them, the walls could be moved easily. One of the missionaries said he always turned on a light when he returned home, just in case his wife had decided to redecorate by moving the walls. Later, Miss Lucy enjoyed living in a lovely Japanese home.

Early in her tour of service in Japan, a Baptist pastor went to her office and asked where she was working on Sunday mornings. He said some young people at his church could benefit from her teaching. She reminded him she did not speak Japanese, but he said the group was interested in learning to speak English. Most of the group were young men. All of the young people were interested in a Bible class.

A US military man had been teaching the class for some time, but he was leaving. Miss Lucy agreed to take the class. She decided if they were really going to study the Bible, she would need an interpreter, so both English and Japanese could be spoken. The group grew. Miss Lucy also met with the group for informal times together. One afternoon when they were to meet Miss Lucy at the park, one of the young men said, "We'll just watch for Miss Lucy's white hair so that we can stay together." Her white hair always fascinated them.

Miss Lucy was always thinking of new ways to give her class more information. Once she asked her interpreter, "What do you think about inviting a few young people at a time to meet so we can sit down with our Bibles and study?" He thought it was a good idea. They decided he would talk to the students about the idea.

Later he told Miss Lucy that some of the Christians

Decision to Go to Tokyo, 1951   59

wanted to attend the small Bible study classes too. Miss Lucy wanted an opportunity to talk with those who were not Christians, but he convinced her the Christians might be of some help. Admittedly, some of them were more interested in learning English than becoming Christians, but the Holy Spirit dealt with all who attended the classes and people were saved. The classes were thrilling and happy experiences.

One night a young man came to the Bible class who had attended before without showing much interest. However, Miss Lucy was interested in him. That night they read the Bible, talked together, and prayed. The young man gave his heart to the Lord. It was a happy occasion for all of them. He asked to speak when they got up from their knees.

"Some months ago, I was standing down here by the Shinjuku station, and a friend of mine got off the train. He asked, 'Have you ever been to this Mejiro Church?'

" 'No, I have never been,' I replied.

" 'Well, you ought to go some time,' my friend encouraged.

"My response was, 'Other people have been telling me about it.'

" 'Take this train to the Mejiro Station. Get off and turn to your left; go a block down that street. Take another left turn. You will see two trees in the middle of the street. (They were planted there by a prince many years ago, but no one would remove them because he had planted them, so they built the street around them.) On the right you will see a building with several doors. Go down the hall, and you will find a woman with white hair who speaks only English,' were the instructions my friend gave.

"Later, I was at that station and I remembered what he told me. I followed his instructions, and everything was as he said. I listened and wanted to forget, but I couldn't. I was irritated with myself because I came, but somehow I felt drawn. Then you started inviting groups into your home. Tonight I know why. Tonight the Lord Jesus has come into my life, and now I am a Christian."

The young man was baptized and later became a deacon in the Mejiro Baptist Church in Tokyo. The Lord works in mysterious ways, and he uses his own people.

In the spring of 1953, Miss Lucy and Johnni Johnson made several trips around Japan to see how the mission work was progressing. They went to Shikoku, which Miss Lucy declared the most beautiful spot in Japan. They visited with the pastor's family in Takamatsu and were pleased with that church's activities. In Tokushima they held the first Baptist service in that city. From there they attended meetings in Matsuyama. They returned to Tokyo tired but pleased with their observations.

Since Japan was under an army of occupation, Southern Baptist missionaries ministered to the military, as well as the Japanese. American men, women, and children became friends of the Japanese people. Miss Lucy said that, of course, not all of the Americans always did right, but there was far more good among the military personnel than bad. American ships were stationed just offshore. Some American sailors discovered a little Japanese church near the harbor where some of the members spoke English and began attending regularly. One night the pastor asked where they received their biblical training. He learned they were Baptists. He said, "It's wonderful that you can come over here after the war and work together in Christian fellowship with our people." That fellowship continued.

Some of those former sailors became missionaries. Others

served as journeymen and some of their children have served in that capacity. "Only the Lord knows," Miss Lucy said, "just how much good has been done and what those years meant both to the Japanese people and to our own who were stationed there."

The missionaries and the military got together for fellowship and worship. The military offered their chapels for services on Sunday afternoons. Many Japanese attended those services. Some went just to hear the Americans speak, but the results were the same. As a result of that, there are English-speaking Baptist churches in Japan today serving English-speaking congregations.

Miss Lucy and Dr. Connely frequently drove through town, checking on the mission work. On one of these drives, they saw a new building being erected near their office. They watched the progress of the building and wondered what it was going to be. Finally, they learned it was to be a Chinese restaurant. The Connelys and Miss Lucy were very pleased and enjoyed eating there once the restaurant was open. One day a young woman asked, "Is that a nice place where you go?" Miss Lucy was astounded at the question until the woman added, "Well, the name of it is The Forbidden City." Miss Lucy laughed and explained that the restaurant was called that because so soon after the war a Chinese restaurant might not be too popular with the Japanese people.

The US military people who attended the Baptist churches in Japan wanted to do something for the Japanese people they could not do for themselves. One of them suggested, "With all the beautiful mountains here, why can't we find a place and build a mountain retreat where Japanese Christians can meet and study the Bible, like Ridgecrest in the United States?" The Japanese could not fully appreciate the reference to Ridgecrest, but they felt honored that their American friends wanted to give them such a lasting gift. US military people made it possible for the Japanese to find a mountain site, purchase it, and build a camp. It is a lovely piece of land southwest of Yokohama, down on the Izu Peninsula. They called the camp Amagi. From the top of the mountain, there is a lovely view of the area around, including Mount Fuji.

The Japanese building on the mountain was built to be used year round. A fireplace was placed in the big meeting room, but the Americans wondered how to heat the bedrooms. The Japanese suggested using hibachies for heat. The Americans were a little skeptical until they slept in the Japanese beds on the floor with the hibachies nearby. Before retiring, they took a hot *ofuro* (bath in Japanese bathtub), then crawled under their covers and slept peacefully through the night.

Many additions continue to be made there, including rooms for conferences and other rooms as needed.

Miss Lucy continued to devote herself to the mission work. On Sunday morning, September, 1954, she received a cable telling her of her mother's death. She had received a letter telling her her mother had suffered a stroke earlier. The day was already planned. So with a prayer on her lips that she might give a good witness throughout the day, she started out to do what was scheduled. She wrote to Dr. Cauthen, "The Lord was so good and so much nearer and real to me than I had ever dreamed he could be. I went to all six services, did what I was supposed to do in each one of them and got home about 10:05 that night."

Some friends spent the night with her. She called the family Monday morning and learned what Scripture and what hymns would be used in the funeral service. Other friends joined her at her home and had a service honoring her mother, using the same Scripture and hymns. Friends on both sides of the sea remembered Miss Lucy with cables, letters, and flowers.

Miss Lucy enjoyed working with many young people during her years in Tokyo. One story she liked to tell was about young men who went to Japan with the United States Army of occupation. "Two of our young women missionaries noticed the young men. 'Boy met girl' and before long they were gazing into each other's eyes. My house made a nice place for courting. The young women talked to me about the young men, especially when they began to get serious. They knew the young men were not trained to be missionaries, so they really talked it over. The soldiers were discharged and went home. The young missionaries had furloughs shortly after the men left. The two couples got together in the States. One of the men went to the seminary in Fort Worth, and the other went to the seminary in Louisville. Both couples were married. After graduation from seminary, we had two new couples in Japan. Those two couples have proved to be such blessings to the work in Japan."

It was nearing furlough time for Miss Lucy, and as usual she was busy until the day she left. "I was getting ready for a party at my house. I was having my Sunday School class and some other young people come over. The phone rang. I answered and heard someone say, 'Aunt Lucy, this is Robert Price, Dorothy's son.' He was out at Tachikawa on his way to Korea. He had the weekend off and wanted to come to see me. I explained that I was having my Japanese friends over and he was welcome to join us. He came. Never in my life have I seen a person walk into the hearts of people as he did that night. It was mutual. They immediately appreciated one another. Robert said later, 'I wouldn't have missed this for anything.' Some of the young people said, 'When he comes back for R and R we'll take care of him while you are away.' That's what happened. He would go to Tokyo and meet his friends there. He would take other Americans with him.

"Not all of our interesting people were in the military. One young man came to Japan as a missionary. This was a bit unusual because at that time the Foreign Mission Board did not appoint single men as a rule. It didn't take him long to get acquainted. He was to teach in the University. While he was in language school in Tokyo, he went to one of our churches and worked with the young people there.

After a time, the young man got rather lonely. He talked with me about a certain young lady in America he thought a great deal of. He went home on furlough at the same time I was home. He came to see me. He told me again he didn't know what he should do. He wanted to marry this young woman, but she hadn't been to the seminary, a requirement for missionaries. If they married, he would have to resign. When she met the qualifications, they could go back. He asked my opinion, and of course I could express an opinion, but they would have to decide. Several times we visited, but always we talked about whether they should marry. At the end of his furlough, he returned to Japan without her. Now, I was not appointed as a matchmaker, but I could tell they were in love.

"But he returned to the States for her. They were married, waited for her to get the training she needed, and both of them went to Japan as missionaries. She has been a great help to him. Someone asked her one day what she felt her most important job in Japan was. She answered without hesitation, 'Keeping him happy.'"

Miss Lucy received a letter from Dr. Cauthen in December. Portions of the letter said:

"Both in Shanghai, Hong Kong, and in Tokyo, you have rendered a service to the mission which has been very distinctive. You have been a person who has taken care of many things which were urgently needed to be looked after, but which would have been neglected had you not been there. You have been in a position to lend an atmosphere of hospitality and encouragement to every missionary both upon their coming to the field and in their service to the mission.

"I think you know that you are greatly loved throughout all the Orient. There have been requests for you to come to Korea. There have been requests for you to come to Formosa to relieve the treasurers in both those places. We have all the while encouraged your remaining where you are because of the very distinctive contribution you are making in Japan.

"I am glad you are coming on furlough. You will mean much to the churches while you are here."

Miss Lucy returned to the United States in July the following summer (1956).

8
Furlough Interrupted

Miss Lucy came home on furlough in 1956. She was glad to be home with friends and loved ones again. About three months after her arrival in the United States, she attended a meeting in Alabama. She had started out to lunch with friends when she was called to the telephone. Dr. Crawley, the new secretary for the Orient (Dr. Cauthen was now the executive secretary of the Foreign Mission Board), said, "Lucy, we have sad news. Dr. Connely has died. He was on his way to the office after attending a meeting and apparently had a heart attack. Dr. Cauthen and I wanted to talk with you to see if you had any suggestions as to whom we might get to take his place."

After talking a while, he said, "I'll let you know what we decide."

"My friends had chosen a lovely Chinese restaurant, knowing how much I would enjoy it. Normally the food would have been delicious, but that day I could hardly swallow," Miss Lucy said. After lunch they went back to the office. They told her Dr. Cauthen was calling from Richmond.

He said, "Lucy, we have talked it over. Would you go?"

She asked, "What do you mean?"

"There isn't anyone else," Dr. Cauthen said. "It's an important job that has to be done now. Will you just stay a while until we can find someone else?"

Furlough Interrupted

She said, "Of course I will go, but I will have to get a visa."

Miss Lucy already had made plans to go to New Orleans and stay with friends. She went ahead with her plans. The next morning she went down to the Japanese consulate. A young Japanese came out and asked, "May I help you?"

"As far as I know, you are the only one who can," Miss Lucy told him. She explained the urgency of the situation.

"If you will send me your passport, I will see that you have a visa waiting for you when you arrive in San Francisco to board your plane for Japan."

She called her family in Oklahoma City and asked them to send her passport to New Orleans. She returned home to pack. The following news release was sent to the press from the Foreign Mission Board when Miss Lucy returned to Tokyo:

MISS LUCY SMITH RETURNS
TO JAPAN MISSION OFFICE

Miss Lucy Smith, Southern Baptist missionary to Japan who has been in the States on furlough since late July, is flying back to Tokyo on Sunday, October 28, to meet the emergency in the treasurer's office of the Japan Baptist Mission caused by the sudden death on October 23 of Dr. Frank H. Connely, treasurer, Dr. J. Winston Crawley, the Foreign Mission Board's secretary for the Orient, announced today.

Miss Smith formerly served in China where she was associate to the secretary for the Orient and later assistant treasurer of the China Missions. In 1951, after all Southern Baptist missionaries had left Communist China, she transferred to Japan where she has been assistant treasurer of the Japan Mission.

A native of Missouri, she has made her furlough home in Oklahoma City. She was educated at Oklahoma Baptist University, Shawnee, and Woman's Missionary Union Training

School (now Carver School of Missions and Social Work), Louisville, Ky. She was pastor's assistant and educational secretary at Olivet Baptist Church, Oklahoma City, for eight years before her appointment to mission service in 1936.

So, three months after her furlough started, Miss Lucy returned to Japan. Friends saw her off in Oklahoma City; friends met her in Dallas and in San Francisco (where her visa was waiting) and in Honolulu. When she arrived at Haneda Airport in Tokyo, a large group of missionary and Japanese friends welcomed her. After Miss Lucy had been in her new job for awhile, she said, "The welcome which I have received and the assurance of cooperation and prayers from the missionaries and Japanese Baptists have certainly been sources of strength and inspiration to me. Picking up the load and bringing together all the loose ends has not been nearly as hard as it could have been and would have been had it not been for all these friends. Not only have I had the prayers and cooperation of these here in Japan, but also in the homeland."

When Miss Lucy arrived at her Japanese home, the maid had her house clean, the bed made, and water hot for a bath. Early the next morning, Miss Lucy visited Mrs. Connely, who lived next door.

Miss Lucy talked over plans with Dr. George Hays and Mr. Edwin Dozier for scheduling an executive committee meeting. The transition from assistant treasurer to treasurer of the mission was eased by the fact that Dr. Connely had the books in good condition.

Everyone was eager to get the right person for the treasurer's job, but the daily work had to be done and no one could be spared from the job he was already doing. A great many changes had to be made both in Richmond and Japan to formalize Miss Lucy's changed responsibilities. The Japan

Furlough Interrupted 69

Mission recommended a person for the treasurer's job, and the Foreign Mission Board had the responsibility of electing him. The election of a new treasurer called for even more paper work, so getting a new treasurer took longer than anyone had originally thought.

In response to a letter from Miss Lucy to him when Dr. Hays became the new treasurer, Dr. Crawley wrote:

> "Thank you for the fine letter expressing your joy at the election of George Hays to serve as treasurer for Japan. I have found general and hardy approval both there in Japan and here at Richmond for his election.
>
> "I believe it should work out fine for you to leave the field on February 4 as you have planned.
>
> "Let me say again how much all of us appreciate the contribution you have made during this emergency there in Japan."

The short "tour of duty" as interim treasurer for the Japan Mission lasted more than a year.

Miss Lucy returned to Oklahoma City on Friday evening, February 14, 1958. She had business to attend to on Saturday and went to church on Sunday. She was so exhausted she fell into bed that night. The next morning she woke about eight, ate breakfast with the family, picked up the morning paper, and went back to her bed to read. The telephone awakened her at noon. She slept the rest of the afternoon. She laughingly asked if anyone wanted to sit up with her that night since she had slept all day. However, when she went to bed she fell asleep immediately and slept through the night. She admitted she hadn't realized that anyone could get that tired.

After returning to Oklahoma City, Miss Lucy received the following letter:

"Dear Miss Smith:

"At the April Board meeting the following Orient Committee Recommendation was passed: 'That we express appreciation to Miss Lucy Smith of the Japan Mission for her fine service during the past year and a half as treasurer for the Japan Mission in the emergency created by the sudden death of Dr. Frank Connely.'

"I am sure you will be happy to have this word of our deep appreciation for your fine work.

"I trust you are having a fine furlough and getting some much needed rest.

Sincerely,
Louise Jordan
Sec. to Dr. Crawley"

9
Return to Tokyo, 1959

Miss Lucy had written to Dr. Crawley before she left Japan to go home concerning whether she should return to China or Japan at the end of her furlough. The Japan Baptist Convention had asked her to return, and the Mejiro Church wanted her to work full time with them. She admitted that her love for China and the Chinese people was very deep, and the China field was appealing. After much prayer and talking with Pastor Yuya, the deacons of the church, and Dr. Hays, she decided to return to Japan.

After a busy year in the United States, speaking in churches, participating in Falls Creek Assembly in Oklahoma, Ridgecrest, Glorietta, and so forth, Miss Lucy returned to Tokyo, February 20, 1959.

Shortly after Miss Lucy arrived in Japan, some of the young people came to her and asked if she would speak in their church in the pastor's absence. She told them she just couldn't do that. Women didn't speak in the churches in Japan, and she didn't want to offend them. She talked with Mr. Edwin Dozier about it after the young people had insisted. The pastor had sent his daughter with the group to ask her. Mr. Dozier said, "Lucy, you can't tell them no. The Japanese Christians are trying to move forward. If the pastor comes to you in person, you must say yes."

The pastor, Brother Yuya, did come. He offered to get an

interpreter for her. Miss Akiko Endo would be her interpreter. (Mrs. Akiko Endo Matsumura later became vice-president of the Baptist World Alliance.) Brother Yuya was one of the oldest pastors in Japan and had been pastor of this church for a long time.

Brother Yuya had had an interesting experience with the Japanese soldiers. They wanted to take over a sizable piece of property which belonged to him. One just didn't refuse when the Japanese soldiers said they wanted something. He did ask what they would give in exchange. They suggested another plot of land. He was pleased because on one corner of the property they had indicated was a large house with space on the lot to add to the building.

Miss Lucy said speaking in their church was really a blessing to her own life, and others said they were very aware of the Lord's presence as she spoke. After this initial experience, she was invited to speak at the Japanese convention. Miss Lucy modestly refused, but the executive secretary came to her the next day and told her they had been observing American churches where the women participated, and he thought it would be good. He said, "You are older and have had more experience than many of our people. We feel it would mean a great deal to our work and to the women of Japan. Your white hair gives you a prestige that we don't have in Japan."

She asked Akiko Endo to interpret for her again. "It was a frightening experience to stand up there in front of all those Japanese men and women to speak," Miss Lucy recalled. "But it was a wonderful experience to be able to speak through an interpreter with a message from God. Today Japanese women do participate in all the work."

She quoted 2 Timothy 1:7, "For God has not given us a

spirit of timidity, but of power and love and discipline" (NASB). This was one of her favorite Scriptures.

Miss Lucy said, "I don't know whether my speaking that night had anything to do with encouraging Japanese women to participate in church work or not, but if it did I am grateful, and I praise the Lord for the opportunities I've had. Now I realize both of the opportunities came simply because I happened to be there. I was not appointed to be a missionary to Japan as such. I had not expected to make that my life work. I was just doing what seemed to be needed at the moment, and the Lord led in it and blessed it, and I shall forever thank him for it."

One evening Miss Lucy was invited to speak in another church. A Japanese family invited her to have dinner with them before the evening services. The wife prepared the meal while the husband and other family members visited with Miss Lucy.

The man was a samurai and had close connections with the emperor and other government officials. He had a vital part in World War II. He had five swords of various sizes of which he was very proud. Each had a soft leather scabbard. As he showed them to her, he ran his fingers along the blades, telling her about them and what they meant to a samurai to have them. He always wore two swords. He told her of many experiences he had through the years. Then he brought out a silver object about one and one-half inches square. There were two windows on each side. Two of the tiny windows could be opened. On the top, the chrysanthemum, the emperor's seal stood out. He told her it was a replica of a Japanese lantern from the emperor's garden.

"You won't find another one like it I think. When the emperor entertains to honor someone, he always gives a gift, exclusive to that particular occasion. There were fifteen of us one night. He gave each of us one of the little lanterns. There was never another one made. I don't know what happened to the other men or to their gifts. They may have been destroyed, but I have kept mine, and I treasure it very much." He handed it to Miss Lucy and said, "I want you to have it." She treasured it very much because of the sacrifice he made in giving it to her.

When the Japanese people visited in Miss Lucy's home, they recognized the emperor's seal immediately and always asked how she got the little lantern.

One morning Miss Lucy and Pastor Yuya were discussing plans. She called his attention to a couple who had been coming to the church services. They rode bicycles to the services. There was no class for their age. A few days later a young man talked with her about working with the young people. They needed a teacher. She agreed to meet with them on Thursday night of the next week. It was the only free night she had. She told him to see if any of them would be interested.

When the night arrived, twenty-two young people attended. She had expected five or six at best. After that, she could not refuse. She told them she would meet with them once a month. She invited them to meet in her home. Knowing the Japanese were limited in the amount of food they had, she always served a meal. One day a military man gave her a ten dollar bill to buy food for the young people. From time to time others gave her money for food for those classes.

Many times people asked Miss Lucy what she did on the mission field. She laughed and said, "Whatever needed to be done." She was appointed to serve in an administrative capacity. Dr. Rankin and Miss Lucy had not been on the field long when the Sino-Japanese War broke out. They had no idea of how long or of how devastating that war would be. Neither did they know how it would affect their work. They learned from those first days that when a need arose they did what had to be done.

"Many times during those years when I was waiting to go to the mission field, I prayed, 'Lord, either take away this burning desire to go, or give me a place to go.' Many times after I was on the field, I realized I could never do what I was able to do there if I had not had the experiences that I had working in the church and in business all those years," Miss Lucy said.

One of the things all missionaries must do is to fill in for missionaries who are on furlough or moving to other places or other responsibilities. Sometimes missionaries accept extra responsibilities without adequate preparation but are able to make the best of the situations. Once when one of the teachers in charge of the BSU was going on furlough, she asked Miss Lucy to help the young man who would be leading the group while she was away.

The first meeting was a weekend retreat which started on Friday night and ended Saturday night. Miss Lucy could not leave with the group on Friday, so she took an early train the next morning. A group of students met her train and drove her out to the camp. She was told that Mike wanted to talk with her. Miss Lucy had never met him, but she knew he was a student in the Southern Baptist school and that he was a Christian.

Lunchtime came before she had an opportunity to visit with Mike. They went into one of the rooms by themselves to talk. Miss Lucy could tell by his expression that he was troubled about something. He told her that the young people in his church were not following him and that he felt his work was failing. He wanted to serve the Lord, but he didn't know where. They talked a while and finally Miss Lucy said, "Mike, is Jesus real to you?" He looked rather bewildered, and she repeated, "Is Jesus real to you?" Before he answered, she said, "He wants to be as real to you as I am. He is a person, and he wants to be real to you. He is interested in you and knows all the problems you are facing."

He lifted his face and looked at her. "I see it. I've been trying to do it all by myself." He thanked her graciously. The rest of the day he smiled broadly when he met her. At last Jesus was real to him.

Miss Lucy said, "Sometimes all of us need to realize how real God is. To many he is a Spirit so far off we have to search for him, when in reality he is with us all the time."

Thinking back over her experiences through the years, she recalled times God had been very real to her when there was more work to do than she could do alone. People sometimes wonder how missionaries have the time to do all the things they have to do. There are always ways to get the work done. When she moved into the home with Miss Kelley and Miss Johnson, the servants were already trained. With all of her outside work, she could not have managed without them. After Miss Kelley was gone, Miss Lucy had the responsibility of running the house. With all the missionaries and other people who stayed in their home, it was great to have efficient servants. She had an excellent cook. He enjoyed cooking and was proud of the meals he fixed. Miss Lucy helped plan the menus, but the cook did all the shopping. They were never certain how many people would be at the house for any meal, but he always managed to have plenty of good food ready. The other servants were women who helped keep the house clean and the guest rooms ready.

When Miss Lucy returned to China after World War II, her servants had already put her house in order.

Another time she was especially aware of God's presence was in Hong Kong, when she had expected to have a week to set up her house before guests arrived. When she arrived home at 8:00 one night, she received a message that she was wanted in Canton the next morning. The next morning she went down to the bank, ran a few necessary errands, and caught a plane to Canton. While there she learned she had only four or five days before she would have house guests. She did not have a stick of furniture in the house. Missionaries and Chinese friends helped, and she was able to get it done. She had no servants, and she was in an area of Hong Kong where Cantonese was spoken and she didn't speak Cantonese. Friends talked with a woman who had worked with other missionaries. She went to help clean but she couldn't cook. She spoke Mandarin, some Cantonese, a little English, and Wu which was spoken in Shanghai. This was the language Miss Lucy spoke. A cook who spoke only Cantonese was hired, and the other helper interpreted for him and Miss Lucy. They managed to work together well.

In Japan finding household help was harder than it had been in China and Hong Kong, but she always managed to have someone. Over and over, she said, "Great is the Lord, and greatly to be praised" (Ps. 48:1). He always provided her with the help she needed. Miss Lucy was very grateful for the servants who made it possible for her and other missionaries to do the mission work that had to be done. She expressed gratitude for prayer mates and others who had helped in various ways through the years.

Miss Lucy enjoyed her association with the young people of Japan. They were blessings to her life as she was to theirs. In addition to her work in the church, her days were filled with conferences, meetings, correspondence, and anything else that needed to be done. Those five years in Japan passed quickly for her. She had originally gone to Japan for a short time but spent thirteen years of her life there.

Before Miss Lucy took her furlough in 1964, suggestions or hints from different sources kept coming to her about going to Hong Kong when she returned. If she went to Hong Kong, she could finish her work in the Orient as she had begun it—with the Chinese. One weekend a friend visited her in Tokyo. They talked at length, recalling the many varied experiences through the years. Miss Lucy was aware her friend seemed to want to say something that she wasn't saying. Finally, Miss Lucy said, "I can tell you have something you want to say; why don't you just say it?"

Her friend responded, "Well, Lucy, they want you to go to Hong Kong to work in the college there. Dr. Lam and Maurice Anderson both said it would be such a blessing if you could come."

Not having even considered it, Miss Lucy began to mull this possibility over in her mind. After praying about it, she called Dr. Cauthen to see what he thought about it. He said that it seemed to be a good idea and the work certainly could benefit from her being there. After much prayer, she decided she would go to Hong Kong after her furlough in 1965.

10
Hong Kong

Going to Hong Kong in 1965 was almost like going to a new station, rather than returning to a familiar one. Though some of the people with whom she had worked in 1949 and 1950 were still there, she found herself in situations she had not been in before. She was aware of her need for some time to adjust. She had gone with the idea of working with the college, so she started making preparation for her duties there.

Even before World War II, Foreign Mission Board personnel talked about a Baptist college in Hong Kong or somewhere in the South China area. The war came and complicated many things. The University of Shanghai was closed to missionaries by the Communist takeover of China. Hong Kong seemed to be the logical place for a Baptist college if land or already existing buildings were available. The Hong Kong Baptist College was established in 1956 by the Hong Kong Baptist Association, but it didn't have its own campus.

The Hong Kong council had been making more land available by cutting off the tops of mountains and putting the dirt into the sea. They chose a site on top of a mountain for the college, and the excess land was used to make an airport.

When Miss Lucy arrived in Hong Kong, the college was almost finished. For four years the college had been holding classes in a part of Pooi Ching boys' school. They only had room for two or three hundred students, and the boy's school had first choice of classroom space in most cases.

The building was to be completed in the summer of 1966 so that the school could open there in the fall. The students who were graduating in the spring of that year wanted the building finished before their graduation, so they could be the first class to graduate there. Many thought it would be impossible, but some people delight in doing the impossible. The new building was finished in the spring, and faculty and students moved in, happy to have space of their own to do their work.

The first commencement was a memorable occasion. Students and friends climbed the mountain and sat out in the open for the graduation exercises. It was a great beginning for greater years ahead.

In the beginning, Miss Lucy worked primarily with the president of the college and Maurice Anderson. She was extremely grateful that the Lord had made this association possible.

The next year Miss Lucy was asked to teach New Testament at the college. Until then most of her teaching had been in school or in the church. Though she had never taught at a college before, it was a pleasant experience. The subject was required, so Miss Lucy said she took no credit for the large classes. This class was supposed to be taught in English, but she felt the students did not understand English well enough. She did not speak Cantonese. She wanted them to make their grades, but she was much more interested in their understanding the Word of God. It was a challenge, teaching in English to students whose English was limited, but she was able to handle it well. She said, "What a privilege to be able to serve the Lord in this place, at this time." She told her co-workers, "My hope and prayer is that I may live so attuned to the great heart of God that I may be used to help these students."

The college was one of Southern Baptists most interesting institutions in Hong Kong. In the beginning, all the students were Chinese.

One day a beautiful Indian woman knocked at her door. She said, "I want to talk to you about getting my brother into your school."

Miss Lucy asked where her brother lived. She said, "He lives in India, but he begged me to come to ask you about his coming to the college."

Miss Lucy was not able to give her any hope because they could not take him, but he was one of many who heard of the school from acquaintances or in advertisements who wanted to come.

A young man from Jamaica came to her office one afternoon, wanting to enroll for the next semester. Miss Lucy explained it was a Chinese school, and unless he spoke Chinese he could not take the classes. Because many other English-speaking students requested permission to attend, arrangements were made to include them.

Miss Lucy interviewed students and met with other people coming in for information. She entertained the visitors and made arrangements for interviews with others when she did not speak their language. She met many lovely people and enjoyed the close relationship with other faculty members.

Miss Lucy had an apartment near the college. She invited students and faculty members to visit from time to time in her home.

Someone asked Miss Lucy if she had ever eaten snake. She shuddered and said a definite, "No." Several weeks later at a faculty dinner, everyone was enjoying a good Cantonese meal. A teacher asked Miss Lucy, "Do you know what you are eating?" They all listened as she gave a negative answer. The teacher said, "It's snake; isn't it delicious?" Everyone laughed, and she joined them. But the food seemed to taste a little different after that, even if it was her imagination.

Miss Lucy loved the association with the students. Most of the young men were very anxious to learn about the New Testament, but some took the course only because it was required. Some of them could understand, but some of the students had no concept of Christianity at all. Miss Lucy took advantage of every opportunity to tell them about Jesus in class and in fellowship time outside of class.

Miss Lucy's report for 1967 was as follows:

> "Another year seems to have rolled around and what has it in the records for us? As I look back I find much for which to be grateful. The Lord has been good and has blessed in so many ways, far beyond anything I have deserved, but he always does that for us. For life, for health, for safety, for a place to serve, for experiences with him and with my fellow-missionaries, as well as the Chinese co-workers, I am very thankful and praise him for all.
>
> "The most interesting thing we can do is to work with people, but it is sometimes hard to be patient and wait until they understand or are ready to move. For the most part my activities this past year have been centered around the Tsim Sha Tsui Mandarin Chapel and Baptist College. The contacts, experiences, and victories won in each place have been enjoyable, but not all that I could have wished they might be. Would we be as faithful if we

were living under the same circumstancs as our Chinese co-workers? I wonder if the Lord is perhaps a bit nearer to them than he is to us, because of some of the experiences which they have had and are now having. Living in a complex society as they do, I am sure the Lord is very real to them. My prayer is that he may be as real to me and I may be able to understand those with whom I work and be of some help to them as we work together day by day.

"It is always a joy to teach the Word of God to those who know him and want to learn more, also to those who do not know him. Both in the Chapel and in the College I have tried to open up some of its truths to the young people in the classes and help them to know Jesus as a real Person, to make him live before them. I have tried to share with them something of what the Word means to me and could mean to them. There has been that thrill which comes to all of us as we see someone accept the Lord as their personal Saviour, follow him in baptism and then serve him. I think all of us in the College have been aware of some 1800 students who have come to us this year and our hearts go out to them as they seek to study and prepare themselves for life as they find it in this day. We covet them each and every one for the Lord.

"Along with the work in the Chapel and in the College, I have tried to help some in other places as needed, have given some help with the *Orient News Sheet,* and also served as a member of the Board of Trustees of the Baptist Press. I have learned more than I was able to give, I know, but have been glad to serve when and where I could.

"The year ahead is as bright as the promises of our

God and so we can press forward in the light of his word and under his direction, assured of more victories.

Soon after Miss Lucy had arrived in Hong Kong, a pastor had asked her to come to his church. He knew she had studied Mandarin, and his was a large Mandarin church on Victoria, the big island of Hong Kong. But he was interested in starting a mission in Kowloon on the other side. The church members of North Point Church wanted to find a place where they could have services for those who lived in that area. Again Miss Lucy was involved with people who wanted to build a church but who were aware of all the problems. To begin with, they found a place to have services on Sunday morning. The space was available for two hours.

Then they found a place that was smaller than they would have liked, but it would suffice. It was downtown near another church which was a Cantonese-speaking congregation. They knocked out walls and did whatever had to be done in order to accommodate the people who came. Members of North Point Church helped all they could. The mission itself took care of most of its own expenses. They were in a great mission field, with a wonderful opportunity to witness.

Most of the churches in Hong Kong were on second and third floors of office buildings. Sometimes apartment houses had a place set aside for services. When they finally found a place they could call their own, they were happy to start plans for getting it ready. Sometimes the job seemed insurmountable, but the Lord could bring joy out of chaos.

When the facilities were ready, they organized their church. It was a thrilling experience for Miss Lucy.

Her church activities gave her opportunity to spend more time with the Chinese people. She had been away from China and Chinese customs for several years, but the people loved her and helped her make the necessary adjustments. She served on many committees, helping set up programs for the church. She said she felt there were times when they had included her in Christian love and courtesy rather than for her help.

At night, Miss Lucy said she would stand and look through the windows at the masses of people and all the hubbub outside. Seeing all the aged, the young people, all ages milling around, made her realize again what a privilege a Christian missionary has to be in the midst of all those crowds and to be able to tell them there is One who loves them, who has a purpose for their lives, and who could lead them to do many things if they would just trust him. So few of them know.

After the church purchased the apartment, a great deal of planning was done to prepare for the dedication service, as well as for the regular program of the church. The dedication was a vital part of getting off to a good start. Big red placards with names on them and beautifully embroidered scarves were used in different places in the apartment. Crocheted scarves were made. All of the flower arrangements had lovely colored bows. Most of the bows were red, but the flowers were primarily white and red. Many of the Chinese pastors and missionaries attended the dedication service. It was a beautiful service, and one they would remember through the years.

Retirement time was approaching. Miss Lucy had acquired quite a library, and she knew she could not take all of those books home with her. One young man had served as an interpreter for her and had been very helpful in many ways. One Saturday when they were preparing for a special meeting, he was helping. To show her appreciation, she gave him two books. He hugged those books to him as if they were a child. He was so pleased to get them. Miss Lucy suggested he might like to come over to look through the books she was not planning to take back to the States with her. He was delighted. She showed him the books and told him to take what he could use. He came in later carrying two sacks full of books and said, "I think I have what I can use."

Later he told her he had put the books on a shelf in his room. When his friends from the seminary asked where he had gotten them, he told them. He gave them permission to read the books, but no one was to take them from the room without his knowledge. He added, "These books will not only be helpful to me, but many others will have the pleasure of using them."

The church kept in touch after Miss Lucy's retirement. The church continued to grow until they were using the whole top floor of the building. With the added room, they were able to have a choir loft. Miss Lucy was surprised and delighted with their use of Negro spirituals. Sometimes the words were translated into Mandarin; at other times they were sung in English.

When she asked why they sang the spirituals so often, they said, "They just say so much. When we sing them, we realize there is a message in them."

The largest Chinese church in the world is in Hong Kong. It is a Cantonese church, but Mandarin and English are also spoken there. The buildings cover a great deal of land, and they have a great program. Their trials through the years have helped them work together.

One such trial occurred in 1949 when there were many fires in Hong Kong. The refugees had built little huts of paper, tin, or whatever they could find. The huts were so close together that if one caught fire several would burn. One afternoon after a meeting at Miss Lucy's, the people were standing outside visiting when someone said, "Look, there's a fire over by the church." One of the men offered to go over and see about it and told Miss Lucy he would come back for her if there was danger of a fire at the church. He did not return immediately, so the group knew the church was safe. She did go with the man later in the afternoon. The whole block looked as if it would burn. People were running everywhere, carrying bedrolls or whatever they could rescue. One of the wealthy families in the church had a large home in the area. The gardens and grounds surrounding the house were beautiful. This family opened the gates and invited people to put their salvaged belongings there and spend the night. Some of the young people from the church prepared food for all those people who had nowhere to go. The compassion and concern they had for one another was an inspiration to all.

Most of the people in Hong Kong had known suffering either on the mainland during the war years or after arriving in Hong Kong just trying to get the necessities of life. When the time came that they did fare better, they showed their gratitude in service. Thus the church has grown and ministered through the years.

Just three months before time for her to come home, the wife of one of the missionaries became seriously ill. The couple had to return home, leaving their work. Miss Lucy took on his job as treasurer in addition to her other office work and her duties at the college. It took a lot of time and effort, but Miss Lucy said, "The Lord always provides."

In the midst of it all, she was sitting in her room one day when she received a call from her sister, Effie Katherine in America, saying her husband had just died. Miss Lucy offered to come home, but Effie Katherine insisted she stay until she completed her tour of service.

11
Retirement

Retirement was not easy for Miss Lucy because she had mixed feelings. She realized she was not just leaving Hong Kong, but her beloved Orient. She realized God still had a plan for her life, and so she looked with anticipation toward a new area of service back in America.

Pearl Johnson, a friend of Miss Lucy's who was also retiring, met her in Hong Kong so they could travel to the States together. They decided to take the long way home, through Singapore, Thailand, Israel, and parts of Europe. It was a delightful way to close their ministries in the Orient, visiting with other missionary friends and observing the work that was being done in new areas of the Orient.

Among the things Miss Lucy and Miss Johnson enjoyed most during their visit in Israel was the trip to the caves in Qumran where the Dead Sea Scrolls had been discovered.

From Israel, the two missionaries traveled to Ruschlikon, Switzerland. The seminary there was one of the highlights of their trip home. They had a brunch in the parlor with both faculty and students attending. Delicious food and coffee were served. They had met a couple in Nazareth who told them their children were in the seminary in Ruschlikon. The first morning, the young couple rushed in to meet them. They asked about their parents and were happy to visit with someone who had just seen them. After graduation, the young couple went back to Israel. They went back to the family shop to work, but their primary work is teaching others about Christ.

In Austria, they toured the beautiful Schönbrunn Castle in Vienna. The furnishings were magnificent as were the grounds. The well-manicured gardens were lovely.

In Iran, they went to the Glass Palace. Many kinds of glass were displayed, tiny prisms radiating the rays of the sun sparkled everywhere. The little glass chimes made light, tinkling sounds. While in Iran they saw many of the Shah's possessions, including the famous Peacock Chair. There were numerous jewels for them to see.

Arriving in New York was a happy experience because it meant going home. Always the best part of any journey is getting home again. A large crowd at the airport welcomed Miss Lucy home. It was a great occasion to see so many loved ones there to greet her.

Two weeks after her return, she was invited to Richmond for her retirement dinner. The Bagbys from Brazil, Pearl Johnson and Miss Lucy from the Orient, and others were honored at the dinner. They were given pins for their years of service. Being a missionary emeritus somehow lacked the thrill of being a new missionary going out. Yet Miss Lucy felt great joy for the privilege of serving the Lord in the Orient for thirty-two wonderful years, through the difficulties and heartaches of three wars. She could say with the apostle Paul, "I have fought the good fight, I have finished the course, I have kept the faith; in the future there is laid up for me the crown of righteousness, which the Lord, the righteous Judge, will award to me on that day; and not only to me, but also to all who have loved His appearing" (2 Tim. 4:7,8, NASB).

Miss Lucy's work for the Lord didn't stop with her retirement. She continued to inspire many people with her love and her service to others.

After Miss Lucy returned home from the Board meeting in Richmond, she received a letter from Dr. Cauthen that expressed what many others felt. A portion of the letter follows:

> "It was a great delight to have you here, and you brought blessing to everybody by your presence.
>
> "You have had a very distinguished missionary career, and we have admired your service, courage, faith and ability more than you know.
>
> "You have the capacity of meeting difficult and critical situations with calmness, poise and insight. You have also shown the capacity to adjust to new places and situations even though the conditions were very different from those you had known in former locations. Your going to Japan and winning such a place in the hearts of those people, was in my judgment, an outstanding demonstration of missionary quality.
>
> "You can look back across the years with that deep satisfaction of a job well done in the service of our Lord and can know that the years ahead will hold rich opportunity to share out of your broad experience many blessings with people here. Some of the finest work that has been done for foreign missions has been accomplished by those who have returned from the fields and have shared with others the reality of our Saviour's promises and blessings."

Retirement for Miss Lucy meant only retirement from active duty on the mission field. After returning to Oklahoma City to live, she taught in schools of missions; appeared on

Retirement

programs and taught classes at the assembly at Falls Creek; served as hostess at the GA camp, Nunny Cha Ha; taught in other GA camps and wherever she was needed. She served as president of the WMU in Olivet Baptist Church and spoke in many churches during weeks of prayer. She taught an adult Sunday School class at Olivet for several years. There seemed to be no limit to what she was willing to do.

In February 1980, the doctors discovered that Miss Lucy had a malignancy. Through her surgery and through all the months afterwards, her sweet Christian spirit was an inspiration to those who did not know her, as well as to those of us who did know and love her.

What a joy it must have been for her when she received letters like this one from Dr. and Mrs. Cauthen:

> "It certainly has been a joy to work with you through the years, in Shanghai, Tokyo, Hong Kong and all the other places of service where our lives have crossed in the service of our Lord.
>
> "When I think of the critical days when communists were bidding for ascendency in China, and we had to take emergency measures, I always experience a great feeling of gratitude for you and for the resourcefulness, courage, dedication, and ability that you demonstrated repeatedly.
>
> "Your going from Shanghai to Hong Kong to open the office was a monumental step, and the Lord blessed it in a remarkable way.
>
> "The days in Shanghai when you, Frank Connely and I along with Elizabeth Ward, were so constantly in prayer and consultation as the storm clouds gathered, revive memories that are very precious indeed.

"Although you did not speak the Japanese language, you made yourself so effective in Tokyo and throughout Japan that the missionaries and the Japanese felt so much the depth of your love and your encouragement that your presence there was a major factor in helping to extend work for Christ."

One who knew her well said, "More than letters of appreciation, Miss Lucy will have the glorious privilege of meeting many people in heaven who are there because of her influence. What joy will be hers to hear the Master's 'Well done, thou good and faithful servant' " (Matt. 25:21).

12
Going Home

On May 27, 1981, God looked down from heaven and said, "Lucy, now it is time to come home," and she went to be with him.

At her memorial service, the lovely floral tribute and the crowded church gave evidence of the love her friends had for her.

The Reverend Ralph Crawford, her pastor, read from Revelation 14:13.

> And I heard a voice from heaven, saying, "Write, 'Blessed are the dead who die in the Lord from now on!'" "Yes," says the Spirit, "that they may rest from their labors, for their deeds follow them" (NASB).

Miss Jaxi Short, missionary from China, said in her tribute, "Lucy was in Shanghai as the missionaries were coming back to China following the [Sino-] Japanese War, and she was there to welcome each one who came. Each one was a special individual. She was there to care for the many needs of the people who were out in the hinterland.

"In 1949 Lucy left China to go to Hong Kong to establish an office there. She was there to extend hospitality to those coming out of Communist China.

"Today, also, Lucy has gone on ahead, and she will be there to meet us when we see her in glory."

Miss Short said that six words came to her mind in thinking of Miss Lucy's life: commitment, compassion, consecration, consideration, concern, and inspiration.

The pastor said, "She knew how to live because she knew what life was all about."

Certainly, she knew how to die. What a glorious privilege to have known her.

Epilogue

Miss Lucy read the first eleven chapters of this book in manuscript form before her death. She said, "I want to add a word before the book is finished":

"All those years I was waiting for a place to serve in the mission field, I wondered why the Lord had called me and helped me prepare with no place to go. Many times while I was in the Orient I knew there were things I had to do that I couldn't possibly have done without the experiences I had while in the business world, teaching, and the years I worked in the church. The Lord always knows what's best and will lead us if we will follow him.

"I will never be able to thank my sister, Effie Katherine, and the family for the way they have taken care of me in this last illness. Not only they but also friends and loved ones at the church, missionaries, national co-workers in China, Japan, and Hong Kong who have written and called. Their concern meant so much to me during those long hours. Now that I am better, I want to say thank you. 'Great is the Lord, and greatly to be praised' (Ps. 48:1). I praise him now for giving us family and friends to take care of us. To Lois Roberts and Elizabeth Smith and others getting the material for the book together, accept my deep abiding love and gratitude. May the Lord bless them all their lives."